Barbed Wire
The Fence That Changed the West

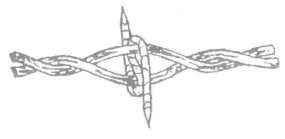

JOANNE S. LIU

Mountain Press Publishing Company
Missoula, Montana
2009

LIBRARY OF CONGRESS CATALOGING-IN-PUBLICATION DATA
Liu, Joanne S., 1971-
 Barbed wire : the fence that changed the West / Joanne S. Liu.
  p. cm.
 Includes bibliographical references and index.
 ISBN 978-0-87842-557-0 (pbk. : alk. paper)
 1. Barbed wire—Social aspects—West (U.S.)—History. 2. Barbed
wire—Political aspects—West (U.S.)—History. 3. Wire fencing—
West (U.S.)—History. 4. Frontier and pioneer life—West (U.S.)
5. Ranch life—West (U.S.)—History. 6. Social conflict—West
(U.S.)—History. 7. West (U.S.)—History. 8. West (U.S.)—Social
conditions. 9. West (U.S.)—Race relations. I. Title.
 TS271.L59 2009
 978'.02—dc22
                                                         2009032922

PRINTED BY DATA REPRODUCTION COMPANY IN THE UNITED STATES OF AMERICA

Mountain Press Publishing Company
P.O. Box 2399
Missoula, Montana 59806
(406) 728-1900
www.mountain-press.com

This book is dedicated to Keishi and Dani.
With you every day is a party.

Contents

Acknowledgments

I n writing and putting this book together, I became indebted to many individuals and organizations. Thanks and appreciation are very much in order:

. . . to Frontier Times Museum, in Bandera, Texas, for opening up the world of barbed wire history to me, and to Jim Tarbox, of *History Channel Magazine*, for being the first to allow me to write about it.

. . . to my editor, Beth Parker, for taking on this project and for making this book a reality. Thank you for your calm demeanor and all your suggestions, honesty, and insistence.

. . . to Gwen McKenna, history editor at Mountain Press, for helping with this project in the last stages and greatly improving the book.

. . . to all my invaluable sources—particularly Gerald Brauer, Paul H. Carlson, Mary Emeny, Harold Hagemeier, Ron Harpelle, Alan Krell, Dain Rakestraw, Earl Hayter, Delbert Trew, Henry D. and Frances T. McCallum, Warren Stricker, and Kathy Vance Siebrasse—whose insight and resources made this book so much better.

. . . to the museums and organizations—especially Devil's Rope Museum, Antique Barbed Wire Society, Ellwood House and Museum, Glidden Homestead and Historical Center, Kansas

Barbed Wire Museum, Panhandle-Plains Historical Museum, and XIT Museum—that keep barbed wire history alive.

. . . to Mark Mitchell, who provided valuable feedback when the idea of the book was the only part that existed.

. . . to my writing buddies—Martha Miller, Terri Schexnayder, and Jane Sevier—who provided the laughs, encouragement, critiques, and curiosity in my work.

. . . to my parents, who showed me what love means. You have guided me every step of the way and I thank you for your sacrifice and support.

. . . to Keishi, who is the only person in the world I want to spend the rest of my life with. Thanks are not enough for traveling down this path with me. You are the one who first said I could do it. You deserve as much credit for this accomplishment as I do. Without your support, I could neither have started nor finished this project. Thank you for your belief in me, and your patience through it all.

I owe thanks to many more individuals who are not mentioned here. A few of them helped me retain my sanity during stressful times, while others lent their support and encouragement.

98th Meridian

Edmonton

ALBERTA

Calgary

SASKATCHEWAN

Regina

MANITOBA

ONTARIO

Winnipeg

MONTANA

NORTH
DAKOTA

Fargo

MINNESOTA

Billings

R
o
c
k
y

M
o
u
n
t
a
i
n
s

SOUTH
DAKOTA

Sioux Falls

WYOMING

IOWA

Cheyenne

NEBRASKA

Omaha

Lincoln

Denver

COLORADO

Kansas
City

KANSAS

MISSOURI

Wichita

OKLAHOMA

Tulsa

Oklahoma
City

ARKANSAS

NEW
MEXICO

Roswell

Lubbock

Fort Worth

TEXAS

LOUISIANA

MEXICO

0   200   400
              miles

The Great Plains (present-day state boundaries shown).
—COURTESY OF THE CENTER FOR GREAT PLAINS STUDIES,
UNIVERSITY OF NEBRASKA–LINCOLN

Chapter 1
Wide Open Range

The landscape of the American West was once dominated by grass. Across the Great Plains, grasses stretched as far as the eye could see, with few trees to interrupt the wind's progress. In many areas, the grass grew so tall that the only way a person could survey the surroundings was to stand up on a horse's back. Frederick Law Olmsted, the famed American landscape architect who designed New York's Central Park, journeyed through Texas in 1857 and described the prairie grasses as moving "in swells like the ocean after a great storm" whenever the wind swept over the land.

The vast grassland was not only windy but dry, with few springs or streams. Any water on the ground tended to evaporate quickly. While the prairies had enough moisture to support limitless stretches of grasses, water was too scarce for forests to take root. Where trees were found on the plains, they usually grew in scattered clusters. For example, cottonwood and elm congregated close to rivers. In Montana and Wyoming Territories, a few isolated forests grew among hills, mountains, and buttes. And central Texas and Oklahoma supported mesquite and oak savannah.

In this grassy region, great herds of American buffalo, or bison, roamed. Until the mid-1860s, the herds numbered in the millions.

To prosper in such numbers, buffalo depended on the vast grasslands of the plains. When a herd depleted a grazing area, it moved on, not returning until the grasses grew tall and abundant again.

Native Peoples

Long before settlers ventured into the American West in the 1840s and 1850s, various Indian tribes inhabited the land. Among these were the Plains Indians, members of at least twenty-eight different tribes scattered throughout the Great Plains, the Southwest, and even parts of the Pacific Northwest.

As early as the mid-1500s, however, European explorers, traders, and trappers had brought diseases that sickened and killed many Native Americans. Over the next three hundred years, cholera, measles, rubella, smallpox, and other illnesses caused significant destruction to tribes in both the East and the West. By the mid-1800s, the overall Indian population had undergone a severe reduction.

Meanwhile, many tribes were moved onto reservations designated by the federal government. Beginning in the 1830s, the federal government began to relocate tribes east of the Missouri River to land it had set aside as Indian Territory, comprising much of the land west of the Mississippi. During the 1850s, 1860s, and 1870s, western tribes were likewise forced onto reservations.

Until then, however, most Plains Indians continued to wander the American West, traveling long distances to hunt and trade. The prairie provided abundant food—herds of buffalo, as well as pronghorns, deer, elk, rabbits, prairie dogs, and wolves. To sustain their traditional way of life, Plains Indians required the open range for hunting, particularly buffalo. The American buffalo, North America's largest land mammal, was the primary source of food, clothing, and shelter for Native Americans on the prairie. Many tribes—including the Apache, Arapaho, Blackfoot, Cheyenne, Comanche, Crow, Kiowa, and Sioux—tracked and hunted buffalo over hundreds of miles.

Cattle Country

Buffalo were not the only herds roaming the West. By the time settlers arrived on the plains, cattle were a common sight, especially in Texas. Western cattle were descendants of longhorn cattle brought to the Caribbean Islands by Spanish conquistadors in 1493. These island cattle were often left loose, and over time they developed the temperament and skills necessary for survival. They grew lean and tough, with their long, sweeping horns proving the ideal weapon against other cattle and predators.

Several decades after the first Spanish conquistador brought longhorn cattle to the Caribbean, a Spanish sea captain illegally brought some of the animals to Mexico. Others soon followed suit, and longhorns became North America's first cattle population. The cattle, allowed to run loose in the new wilderness, eventually drifted north, entering the United States through present-day Texas and California in the 1500s.

Back East, Europeans brought different cattle breeds from England. The Devon, for example, was one of the earliest breeds, arriving in Massachusetts in 1623, while the shorthorn arrived in Virginia in 1783. The Hereford was first brought to Kentucky in 1817, and the Angus came to Kansas in 1873.

Starting in the 1820s, cattle of mostly English and northern European stock had been brought into the West, including Texas, by Americans from the East and by immigrants from Europe. Before long, however, these early cattle owners discovered that eastern cattle were not hardy enough to survive on the harsh prairie. As beef became more popular in the United States, American entrepreneurs began to eye the half-wild western longhorns with dollars in mind. But longhorn meat was tough and unappetizing to American consumers.

The answer—to blend east and west—at first happened naturally as the cattle interbred and the strongest traits were passed on. Later, cattle breeders refined the mix. From the blending of

Texas longhorn. —BUREAU OF LAND MANAGEMENT

Anglo and Spanish cattle emerged a new hybrid breed, the Texas longhorn. Known for its hardiness, the Texas longhorn could subsist in harsh country where no other breed could survive for long. By the mid-1800s, the Texas longhorn was the predominant breed in the American West.

Cattlemen and Cowboys

As settlers began to arrive on the plains to farm, they found, along with cattle, cattlemen and cowboys. These inhabitants, who hardly considered the land an unexplored desert, already held a commanding presence in the West. From the mid-1800s, as the demand for beef increased, the cattle business dominated more and more of the western economy. Having started in the Southwest, especially Texas, the American cattle industry was expanding northward into the excellent grazing lands of the Great Plains at the same time as farming homesteaders began pouring in after the Civil War.

The average cattle owner, or cattleman, owned hundreds of head of cattle, and some herds numbered in the thousands. Cattlemen hired cowboys to carry out most of the daily cattle-raising operations. Cowboys, typically men in their early twenties but sometimes as young as twelve or thirteen, handled the livestock. They spent hours in the saddle, constantly herding cattle to new grazing and watering areas, riding after loose cattle, and watching for predators such as mountain lions and coyotes.

Many of the techniques used by cowboys of the mid-1800s came from Mexico, where cowboys were called *vaqueros*. Vaqueros,

Through the 1800s, cowboys tended cattlemen's livestock on the open range. This cowboy on horseback herded cattle on the Sherman Ranch in Genesee, Kansas (c. 1902).
—NATIONAL ARCHIVES AND RECORDS ADMINISTRATION

whose origins dated back to the mid-1600s, first arose when an overabundance of loose cattle throughout Mexico called for killing the animals. Vaqueros were hired to accomplish the gruesome task. Regarded as little more than poor laborers on horseback, they spread throughout the Spanish empire, gradually extending into its northern reaches, now known as Texas.

In the early 1800s, Euro-American cattle-raisers, mostly from the South, started to migrate into the West. Before long, the Anglo cattle-herders began to absorb some of the Spanish cattle-raising culture, resulting in the American cowboy. Spanish vaqueros taught their Anglo counterparts how to round up cattle, bring down a steer, and break a wild bronco. The vaqueros also influenced the dress and lingo of cowboys. Before long, the peculiar practices and customs of the cowboy were ingrained throughout the West's cattle-herding culture.

Cattlemen and cowboys sometimes had conflicts with the native inhabitants of the West. Members of the more aggressive tribes sometimes raided ranches, cattle trains, and cowboy camps to steal livestock and supplies. Generally, however, Indian tribes coexisted relatively peacefully with cattlemen and cowboys. Like the buffalo, cattle required limitless stretches of grasses to graze on. Since the survival of both Indians and cattlemen depended on the vast grasslands of the region, the two groups shared a common interest in the open range. By the time the postwar migration of eastern settlers began, the cultures of the natives and of the cattlemen were well established. The newcomers would have much to learn.

The Law of the Open Range

Western cattle country had strange traditions. According to the Law of the Open Range—an unwritten rule that reigned in the West—cowboys and cattle traveled freely across the land, with unimpeded access to grass and water. The open range rule had evolved out of the federal government's practice of allowing cattlemen to graze their livestock on public lands. As cattle grazing on public lands proliferated, the practice eventually extended to undeveloped, privately owned land.

Unlike in the East, where private property rights ruled, in the West it did not matter who legally owned the land. Cattlemen and their cattle had the right to use any water or grazing pastures they pleased. In fact, a cattleman might own ten thousand head of cattle yet not own one square inch of land. The Law of the Open Range was a given, a way of life that no one in the West questioned.

"The Great American Desert"

As late as the mid-nineteenth century, Americans who studied a map of the United States might find, in big, bold letters, "The Great American Desert—Unexplored" marked across much of the area

Approximate boundaries of "The Great American Desert." In the first half of the nineteenth century, most Americans believed this region was a virtual wasteland. Maps during this period differed over the region's precise boundaries, but most depicted the "desert" extending west from the Mississippi River to the eastern edge of the Rocky Mountains.

between the Mississippi River and the Rocky Mountains. Believing the western frontier to be uninhabitable—or at least unsuitable for farming—most Americans never ventured west of the Mississippi. In fact, in 1840 fewer than 700,000 of the nation's 17 million citizens speckled the western landscape. The majority of Americans crowded the Northeast, South, and eastern Midwest.

In 1803 President Thomas Jefferson supposed the western frontier to be "immense and trackless deserts." Other prominent figures, such as author Washington Irving and explorer Zebulon Pike—after whom Pikes Peak is named—made similar dismal declarations, shaping Americans' impression of the West well into the 1850s. Most Americans were reluctant to part with the conveniences of long-established communities and challenge the desolate terrain beyond the Mississippi.

"Go West, Young Man"

In spite of the frontier's ominous reputation, the notion of settling the West had its advocates. Starting in the 1840s, American business and government leaders promoted the alluring idea of Manifest Destiny—that the United States was destined to extend from the Atlantic to the Pacific, which of course included the inland West. As the earliest settlers took off for Oregon Territory in the 1840s, they discovered that the Great American Desert was not really a desert. Though water was scarce in places, the vast expanses of rolling grasses showed settlement potential after all. The phrase "Go west, young man," attributed to John L. Soule, first appeared in 1851 and became something of a national motto urging people to set their ambitions on the unsettled West.

Yet even into the 1860s, the West remained largely unpopulated. West of Missouri, settlers found themselves straddling the end of civilization and the beginning of the frontier. Those who dared to venture forth encountered wild country without adequate water sources, making the establishment of self-reliant communities on the plains a trying task. Before the Civil War, most would-be settlers went to the more bountiful lands of the West Coast—California, Oregon, and Washington Territory. The few who tried to make a go of it inland found the going mighty tough. For example, in 1860, 30,000 settlers abandoned Kansas Territory because of a severe drought.

Nevertheless, Soule's words continued to linger in American minds into the pre–Civil War years, and many people considered heeding the call, for the West offered opportunities and independence found nowhere else. As mainstream Americans realized that the West was far from a wasteland, they began to look upon the unbounded stretches of open land as an invitation to settle.

Chapter 2

In the Wake of War

The American Civil War, from 1861 to 1865, delayed the country's expansion into the West. As violence overtook the nation, Americans focused on survival, postponing thoughts of adventure and opportunity on the frontier. Men fought either to preserve or to splinter the union while women and children eked out a living as best they could and waited for their men to return home.

Nevertheless, even as the divided country threw its energy into fighting the war, an entirely different view of the West was evolving. By the end of the war in 1865, cartographers would replace "The Great American Desert" with "The Great Plains" on their maps.

The change in notation reflected a critical advancement in Americans' knowledge of what lay west of the Mississippi River. This knowledge, in turn, created a dramatic shift in attitude. During the war years, more and more people were learning that the soil of the Great Plains was, in fact, excellent for farming crops such as wheat and corn. What was once supposed a vast wasteland was now lauded as the next frontier for enterprising souls, a land of limitless opportunity. As the nation began its recovery from the war, Americans grew increasingly interested in moving westward. "Rain follows the plow" became a popular expression

Civil War ambulance crew removing wounded soldiers from the battlefield (early 1860s).
—COURTESY OF THE LIBRARY OF CONGRESS, PRINTS AND PHOTOGRAPHS DIVISION
(REPRODUCTION NUMBER, LC-DIG-CWPB-03950 DLC)

among war-weary Americans hopeful about the farming potential of the Great Plains.

A Nation in Turmoil

Though much of the Civil War fighting occurred in the East, its repercussions reverberated deeply throughout the nation, including the West. White frontier settlements that had sprouted up before the war were left on shaky ground. The removal of federal troops from the frontier to the war front had created disorder. Settlers could no longer rely on soldiers to defend them from outlaws and Indian raids. With this weakened military presence, some displaced native tribes recognized an opportunity to try to move back into their former homelands and hunting grounds. Comanche and Kiowa bands in New Mexico Territory, Indian Territory (which by the 1860s would be limited to what is now Oklahoma), and Texas, in particular, were able to deter white settlement and reduce Anglo populations during the war years.

Not only did the federal government do little to assist with Indian problems in the West during the war, but after the war it banned settlers from forming local militias, fearing that such local forces in previously Confederate-controlled areas might renew their fight against the Union. With so little government support, some western soldiers and civilians took the law into their own hands and killed any Indians—hostile or not—who crossed their paths.

After the war, the federal government concentrated its efforts in those western states and territories that had fallen under the control of the Confederacy—including New Mexico, Indian Territory, Kansas, Texas, and Arkansas—and focused on asserting its authority over troublemakers sympathetic to the Confederacy rather than over outlaws, vigilantes, and aggressive Indians. It was not until a year after the war's end that the government gradually began establishing federal forts to protect settlers and force Native Americans back to their assigned lands.

Postwar frontier violence was not limited to conflicts between whites and Native Americans. The emancipation of slaves created an influx of black families into the West, contributing to the disorder. Many white westerners resented the migration of former slaves onto their turf. Intimidation and even murder was not uncommon.

Cattle Chaos

The upheaval of the war also disrupted businesses, including the cattle industry. The army recruited most of the cowboys who normally managed the livestock. Cattle in the West, so highly prized and carefully tended in times of peace, were, during the war years, largely left to their own devices. For the most part, the herds simply roamed without restraint, supervision, or accounting. Although they multiplied and grew fat on the teeming grasses all on their own, thousands of cattle remained unbranded, making it virtually impossible to identify their owners. But few cattle owners had the resources to drive and ship livestock to markets anyway, as most Americans could not afford beef in the wartime economy. The cattle market languished.

When the Civil War ended, cattlemen and cowboys began sorting out the livestock. In Texas alone, more than five million cattle were found wandering free, unbranded, and ignored. But the cattle's roamings were in keeping with the Law of the Open Range. In wartime or peace, nothing could interfere with this age-old tradition of the West.

Hungry for Beef

As peace returned and Americans turned their attention back to commercial pursuits, factories sprang up and people went back to work. Families could now afford to put beef on their tables. The cattle industry began to flourish again, soon becoming a key component of the national economy.

In addition to the return of general prosperity among Americans, the federal government helped to fuel the demand for beef. In the late 1860s, when the U.S. military began to expand federal forts in the West to subdue the Indians who were threatening

Branding calves and mavericks kept cowboys busy during roundups (South Dakota, 1888). —COURTESY OF THE LIBRARY OF CONGRESS, PRINTS & PHOTOGRAPHS DIVISION (REPRODUCTION NUMBER LC-DIG-PPMSC-02632)

settlers, the soldiers had to be fed, and the army turned to beef. The demand for cattle exploded into undreamed-of proportions. The price of beef skyrocketed. A Texas steer worth four dollars before the war now commanded forty dollars in northern markets such as Chicago and Cincinnati.

With the boom, cattlemen and cowboys across the West dove back into the cattle business. Some cattlemen contracted with the government to supply beef to frontier forts as well as Indian reservations in parts of Texas, Indian Territory, and New Mexico Territory. But most cattlemen drove their cattle to the railroads for shipment to markets in the East.

In the meantime, however, huge herds of unbranded cattle still wandered the open range, and less honest men recognized an opportunity for substantial profits. Thieves and rustlers, enterprising businesspeople, and displaced army veterans started their own herds by gathering unmarked cattle and mavericks and branding them with their own brands. Some rustlers went so far as to steal branded cattle and alter the brands. Up until the mid-1860s, rustling had been an infrequent infringement. After the Civil War, though, many opportunists seized the moment.

Rustling was costly for legitimate cattlemen. To prevent the crime, some cattle owners hired men whose sole job was to protect herds. Others hired detectives to aggressively expose rustlers. When they caught up with the thieves, cattlemen sometimes exacted their own justice with an impromptu hanging intended to send a message to other rustlers.

Trail Drives

As the price of cattle rose, cattlemen and cowboys doubled their efforts to get their cattle to market. Twice a year, they rounded up their livestock for the trail drive, which meant moving herds over thousands of miles. In spite of the time and labor involved, drives were the only viable way to transport beef to market. Some cattlemen sent their cowboys to drive cattle directly to various western

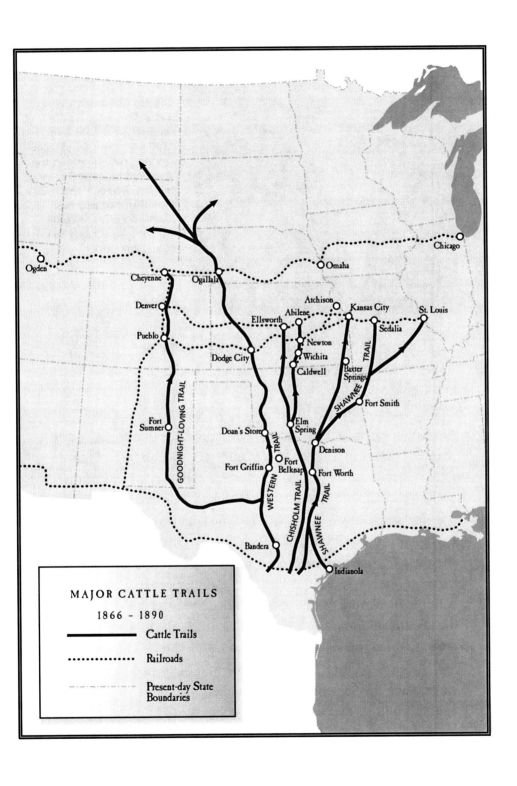

Ogden

Chicago

Cheyenne
Ogallala
Omaha

Denver
Atchison
Abilene
Kansas City
St. Louis

Pueblo
Ellsworth
Sedalia

Newton
Dodge City
Wichita

Caldwell

Baxter
Springs
SHAWNEE TRAIL
Fort Smith

GOODNIGHT-LOVING TRAIL

Fort
Sumner
Doan's Store
Elm
Spring

WESTERN TRAIL
Denison

Fort Griffin
Fort
Belknap
Fort Worth

CHISHOLM TRAIL
SHAWNEE TRAIL

Bandera

Indianola

MAJOR CATTLE TRAILS

1866 – 1890

———— Cattle Trails

·············· Railroads

Present-day State
Boundaries

Charles Goodnight, who was responsible for blazing the first cattle drive in 1866 along the Goodnight-Loving Trail. Goodnight is also credited with inventing the chuckwagon and with founding two ranches in the Texas Panhandle.
—COURTESY OF AMARILLO PUBLIC LIBRARY

forts and settlements, but most were bound for railheads such as Abilene, Kansas, where the stock would be loaded onto train cars and transported east.

Until the transcontinental railroad was completed in 1869, few rail lines passed through the West. Before that time, cattlemen in Texas, the heart of cattle country, had to drive their cattle to New Orleans, the closest port, where they loaded the animals onto ships bound for the Atlantic seaboard. The expense of transporting beef this way was high, and most cattlemen barely broke even. With the railroad, however, the cattle could be taken to the East Coast—as well as to the West Coast and to points in between—much more quickly and relatively cheaply. Combined with the higher prices beef commanded after the war, cattle raising became a profitable venture. All cattlemen had to do was get the cattle to a railhead.

As early as the 1840s, cattlemen in Texas had driven their cattle along the Shawnee Trail to markets in Kansas City, Sedalia, and St. Louis. When settlements increased to the point that the trail was impassable, cattlemen blazed other trails farther west. A railhead for cattle shipping was built in Abilene, Kansas, when the

Kansas Pacific Railroad reached that point in 1867. The drives from Texas to Abilene traveled the Chisholm Trail, one of several famous cattle trails used during the western trail drive's heyday. Others included the Goodnight-Loving Trail, which led to markets in New Mexico and Colorado and eventually to Cheyenne, and the Western Trail, which led to Dodge City and territories in the north.

Cattle trails from Texas, New Mexico, Colorado, and elsewhere eventually extended to Wyoming and Montana. The drives passed through many cities, including Cheyenne, Wyoming Territory; Abilene and Dodge City, Kansas; and St. Louis, Kansas City, and Sedalia, Missouri. In some cases, cattle literally trod through the streets on their way to market. In many ways, trail drives represented the heart and soul of the Law of the Open Range, allowing cowboys to freely drive tens of thousands of cattle across the plains.

Settlers versus the Open Range

With the mounting economic power of western cattle ranching, it became essential to create rules to protect the industry. Cattlemen reinforced the age-old tradition of the Law of the Open Range. They warned newcomers to the West, through word of mouth, posted signs, and direct threats, not to interfere with free grazing or block cattle-driving routes with fences.

But beef wasn't the only food in demand, and settlers turned to the West with an eye to farming. After the war, the nation's growing urban populations in the East increased the demand for grain. During the same period, famine and war conditions in Europe created a need for imported grain from America. Thus, would-be farmers hoping to help meet the demand migrated onto the plains, most of which cattlemen considered open range. With the help of federal legislators, who largely encouraged western settlement, the newcomers began to infringe on the established open range. Before long, enough settlers arrived to severely challenge the traditions of the open range and the cattlemen's way of life.

Chapter 3

Land Up for Grabs

Through the mid-1800s, Manifest Destiny continued to form the basis of the federal government's approach to the West. According to the government's view, persuading Americans to move to and settle the frontier would have several huge benefits. First, to occupy the West was to control it. Second, linking the East and West Coasts would create a stronger union. Finally, an agricultural economy based on farming the fertile lands of the West would allow the nation to be more prosperous and self-sufficient.

President Thomas Jefferson, in 1785, had referred to farmers with reverent words: "Cultivators of the earth are the most valuable citizens. They are the most vigorous, the most independent, the most virtuous, and they are tied to their country and wedded to its liberty and interests by the most lasting bands." Half a century later, the U.S. government began taking action to ensure that a farming economy would become a reality.

Homestead Legislation

As early as the 1840s, the U.S. government began to pass laws to attract people who would, in exchange for land at low or no cost, move west to start farms. In 1841 Congress passed the Preemption Act, which allowed squatters—those who settled on government land without first paying for it—the right to buy the land at a low cost later, after it was surveyed and before it went up for public sale. After living on the land for at least fourteen months they could purchase up to 160 acres for as low as $1.25 per acre.

Support for the idea of granting free land to settlers in the West began to gain momentum after the Mexican-American War, which lasted from 1846 to 1848. The economic prosperity after the war drew large numbers of immigrants to the country, and much of the support for land grants arose from this group, who had little wealth. Moreover, the influx of immigrants in the East created crowded conditions and motivated many Easterners to look westward for land to claim as their own. In addition, people who had already settled in the West became increasingly desirous of more land.

Another early law, the Donation Land Law of 1850, allowed a married couple to claim 640 acres of free land in Oregon Territory if the claimants cultivated the land for four consecutive years. Oregon Territory included present-day Oregon, Washington, and Idaho, along with parts of Montana and Wyoming, but the government quickly extended the land grants to California before the law was set to expire in 1855.

Many land-grant supporters wished to expand the grants to encourage large-scale settlement of the interior West as well as the coastal region. But despite the enthusiasm of many federal legislators, the idea was not popular with everyone. For example, some businessmen in the North opposed the idea, worried that free land would entice away their labor supply, increasing the cost of labor and biting into their profits. Furthermore, free land in the West would increase the supply of available land in the East, lowering their property values.

The South was also a stronghold of resistance to land grants. Many Southern slaveholders were afraid that their slaves would try to flee to the West to claim homesteads for themselves.

Furthermore, if enough former slaves became landowners, they would increase their wealth and thus their political power, significantly boosting the abolitionist cause.

A perhaps even larger concern was that increased farming in the West would compete with the agriculture in the South. In 1861, however, when the South seceded from the Union, a large faction of the opposition disappeared, since delegates from the eleven Southern states were now gone. With the driving force of resistance to the passage of a land-granting act eliminated, the remaining legislators moved ahead with the idea.

The Homestead Act of 1862

In 1862 President Abraham Lincoln signed the Homestead Act, which offered 160 acres of public lands to any citizen or intended citizen who would improve and farm the land for five years. This offer applied primarily to the interior West, since most of the country's undeveloped land lay between the Missouri River and the Rocky Mountains. For many people—such as poor immigrants,

Homestead Act Commemorative Stamp. —COURTESY OF FRED HULTSTRAND
HISTORY IN PICTURES COLLECTION, NDIRS-NDSU, FARGO

unmarried women of limited means, former slaves, tenant farmers—paying an $18 filing fee and committing to five years of work in order to own property was the perfect opportunity to secure a new life. Homesteaders could also choose to purchase land at a low price—$1.25 per acre—after residing on it for only six months and making small improvements to the claim.

After the Civil War, the government rewarded Union soldiers by deducting the time they had served in the army from the residency requirements. Anyone who had "borne arms against the United States, or given aid or comfort to its enemies," however, was not eligible, prohibiting many Southerners from taking advantage of the act. The federal government hoped to settle the frontier with citizens who believed in a unified country or, at the very least, would not take up arms against it.

The Homestead Act remained in effect until 1976 (1986 in Alaska). During the act's existence, the government received nearly four million homestead claims and privatized 270 million acres of public land—10 percent of all land in the country. Although fewer than half of those who claimed homesteads—1.6 million—ultimately succeeded in fulfilling the requirements to earn outright ownership of their claims, the Homestead Act left an indelible mark on the American West.

From All Walks of Life

The promise of free land enticed Americans from all walks of life. Settlers from the East and West Coasts traveled inland to claim a homestead, and farmers in the Midwest crossed the plains seeking more land and greater opportunities. Many of the settlers were former Union soldiers looking for a fresh start. Many were immigrants, some of whom had been struggling in the eastern states.

Other immigrants were new arrivals from France, Germany, Ireland, Italy, Norway, Poland, Spain, Sweden, Yugoslavia, and other countries. Immigrants were generally poor—Europe in the

1860s was rife with war and famine. C. F. Carlsson, a Swedish immigrant who homesteaded in Nebraska, wrote in 1880, "The country is beautiful, if any land on earth deserves to be called so. And if you compare conditions here with Sweden's, there is no similarity at all . . . Your finest plowlands at home cannot compare with the rich prairies here."

Others attracted by the Homestead Act included single women, both never married and widowed. The laws of the time did not usually favor their status, but the Homestead Act offered single women the same deal as men. These women often looked to homesteading as a path to greater independence. Former slaves also recognized the opportunity the act presented. In 1865, many newly freed slaves began heading west to start a new life.

A homestead family migrating to Nebraska in 1886.
—U.S. NATIONAL ARCHIVES AND RECORDS ADMINISTRATION

Although the federal government's intention in passing the act was to enable citizens to own and farm public land, there were those who used the law for other purposes. Many were real estate speculators who planned to sell the land later at a significant profit. Mining speculators made claims in locations they hoped held precious minerals, and lumbermen looked to areas such as Minnesota that were rich in timber. These speculators made minimal efforts to satisfy—or appear to satisfy—the basic requirements of the Homestead Act.

Corporations also circumvented the intention of the act by underhandedly claiming homesteads. Some companies hired individuals to file claims and later transfer the homestead to the organization. Sometimes railroad companies approached struggling homesteaders and offered to buy them out or at least acquire a right-of-way, often at bargain prices. Many desperate claimants felt they had no choice but to agree.

The promise of free land also attracted many individuals with honest intentions. Farmers, especially those who could not afford the price of land in the East, seized the opportunity for free acreage in the West. Others had no background in farming, just high hopes. Most homesteaders—even those who knew how to live off the land—knew little of the traditions of the West, such as the Law of the Open Range, or of the cattlemen, the cowboys, or even the cattle.

The Law of the Open Range versus Herd Law

Settlers from the East and elsewhere knew little of the culture and traditions of the West, but they soon realized their arrival was less than welcomed. Their ambition to transform the prairies and plains into farmland meant cutting up its sea of grasses into a patchwork of carefully cultivated plots. Cattlemen and cowboys were particularly threatened by the barriers homesteaders built around their claims—fences that blocked free passage of stock through the open range.

Homesteaders hailed largely from the East, where fences were a natural part of the landscape. Bringing their own belief system to the frontier, they reckoned that fences would instill structure in the wild and lawless land. In the eastern states, the tradition of Herd Law, which had evolved in regions dominated by a farming economy and with populations much denser than in the West, required that livestock owners fence in their animals to keep them from damaging neighbors' crops.

In the West, however, the Law of the Open Range was the rule, directly contradicting the assumptions behind Herd Law. The idea of fencing land was not only foreign to cattlemen, it threatened their livelihood—cattle needed large, trackless areas to graze and water. On the open range, cowboys led cattle wherever they willed, to any water or grazing areas, regardless of who owned the land.

In some western states and territories, Herd Law custom found its way into law. In Nebraska, the state legislature passed the Herd Law Act of 1870, which required livestock owners to keep their livestock out of other people's crops. Those who failed to do so would be required to pay damages, and failure to pay gave the crop owner the right to keep the offending livestock until the payment was settled. In Colorado, too, Herd Law was legislated.

Yet even where Herd Law was on the books, the laws were not much enforced. Most western cattlemen did not accept Herd Law, and cattle largely still roamed free, so farmers often built their own fences around their crops, finding it more expedient to do so than to rely on cattlemen to restrain their stock. The fact that the laws were generally ignored was an indication of the coming power struggle between farmers and cattlemen.

Ultimately, the group wielding the most power decided who would be responsible for putting up fences. During the 1860s and 1870s, cattlemen, not farmers, held the power all across the West. The livestock market dominated the economy during that time, so the Law of the Open Range dominated the culture. But the balance of power was shifting. By the end of the century, more than 600,000 claims for 80 million acres would be submitted to the federal government. It was only a matter of time before the culture clash erupted.

Chapter 4

Sticks and Stones

As settlers poured into the American West, they staked out 160-acre plots and set to work preparing the land for agricultural use. Homesteaders typically arrived at their claim with much hope but very few possessions. Many lacked the agricultural tools needed to start a farm or the funds to acquire seed and livestock. Facing the unfamiliar conditions and the scarcity of resources such as water and timber on the frontier, settlers worked hard, suffered hardships, and continually sought solutions for unexpected problems.

Accounts abound detailing the hardships and burdens of homesteading. Many found the hard work of homesteading too difficult and abandoned their claims along with their goal of obtaining freehold title to the land. Some settlers left the West altogether. Others hopscotched their way through the West, hoping to stake a claim in a more desirable spot. Among those who stuck it out, most just barely got by.

Whatever their eventual fate, newly arrived settlers had to set to work immediately, building a home out of whatever materials were at hand—often this was sod (bricks of dried mud and grass). They also had to dig a well, prepare the crop fields, and build fences.

Fences

One of the homesteader's first tasks after building a dwelling was to put up some sort of barrier around the property to establish boundaries, restrain livestock, and protect crops. Without fences, livestock and large poultry could wander off, and livestock could trample fields and consume crops. Worse, loose livestock contaminated water sources. Hiring men to continuously herd livestock away from fields and water sources was far too expensive for most farmers. Even if it were affordable, it would be an inefficient use of manpower. A lack of adequate and affordable fencing material, however, proved to be a serious impediment to homesteaders on the plains.

Settlers in the East were used to having plenty of wood available for fencing. But timbered areas were few and far between in the American West. Settlers who came to the frontier before the Civil War typically had their pick of land and could choose prime

A rail fence such as those commonly found in the East (Fort Sanders, Tennessee, 1938). The Great Plains lacked abundant timber or stone, the natural resources typically used for fence building. —U.S. NATIONAL ARCHIVES AND RECORDS ADMINISTRATION

sites with natural water sources and plentiful trees, which they could use to make fences. By the 1860s, however, most of the timbered land was already claimed.

Even when timber was available, wood was not the ideal material for fencing. It rotted in the weather and needed constant repairs, a costly expense. Rail fences were also extremely vulnerable to fire. Prairie fire was an ever-present threat, particularly during droughts, which occurred more frequently on the Great Plains than in other areas of the country.

Settlers from the East were also accustomed to having fields of stones, just waiting to be picked up and assembled into walls. Upon arriving on the plains, they found no such abundance of stones. There were a few exceptions, such as the granite and limestone of the Hill Country in Texas, and the limestone in Kansas and Nebraska.

Limestone walls, if properly built, hardly ever required repair and could remain intact for over a hundred years. But they had many disadvantages. Building a wall out of limestone took a lot

A limestone fence along Kansas State Highway 99.
Settlers dug limestone slabs out of the earth and broke them into smaller pieces before stacking them together to create a barrier.
—COURTESY OF THE KANSAS GEOLOGICAL SURVEY

of time and hard work, and newly arrived homesteaders were already stretched to their limits on both. Building a stone wall also required skill; improperly laid stones could lead to drainage problems and cause erosion. Moreover, a limestone wall took up valuable space in the fields—they were typically three feet wide, and they shaded an even wider area.

With neither timber nor stone in adequate supply, it soon became apparent to plains settlers in the 1860s and early 1870s that they would have to seek out new fencing solutions if they were to successfully settle the region.

Trenches, Ridges, and Hedges

Lacking wood and stone, prairie settlers experimented with various potential fencing options: ridges, ditches, sod bricks, walls of brush and stumps. One rudimentary approach was to dig trenches around the crops. But these furrows inevitably proved sorely inadequate, for most livestock had no qualms about crossing them. To dig ditches deep enough to keep livestock out was too time consuming, and deep ditches would also prevent the farmers themselves from getting to their fields with large tools and equipment.

Another approach was to build dirt ridges three feet or higher. These soil ridges were popular, and like sod houses, they were a common sight on the plains, particularly in Nebraska. But digging dirt and piling it up was hard, time-intensive work. Worse, all the shoveling and heaving produced inadequate results. Ridges were little better than furrows for restraining livestock, which could often climb over the barrier. Furthermore, passing rainstorms could turn ridges muddy and, eventually, flat. From 1850 to 1870, many plains farmers considered hedges the best possible fencing solution, and these living fences became the most popular crop barrier in the region. In fact, it was commonplace for farmers to ask not what was the best fence to use, but what was the best hedge to grow.

Osage orange hedgerows bordering a dirt road in Caldwell County, Kentucky, in 1920. —COURTESY OF KENTUCKY HISTORICAL SOCIETY, WILLARD ROUSE JILLSON PHOTO COLLECTION

After planting, the hedge branches were cut, bent, and intertwined in a technique called plashing to create a barrier impervious to cattle. In the Gulf Coast region—Arkansas, Texas, and Louisiana—settlers favored Cherokee and Macartney rose hedges. But on the Great Plains, most farmers preferred the equally thorny Osage orange hedges, which were, according to the advertisements, "horse high, bull strong, and hog tight." Persistent farmers could grow Osage orange hedges much taller than a horse, up to thirty-five or forty feet high. A thriving industry emerged for hedge seeds and seedlings. Jacob Haish, a German immigrant and Illinois lumberman who would later patent a barbed wire design, fared well selling Osage orange seeds.

Hedges offered more longevity than dirt barriers and required less maintenance. Moreover, when crowded together, hedges could provide a wind and snow break, lessening the ravages of weather across the plains, an advantage that most other barriers could not claim.

Despite their popularity, hedges had clear disadvantages. At five to ten feet in width, hedges took up even more valuable crop space than limestone walls, and they cast a shadow that created an even wider sunless area. In addition, growing and maintaining hedges required a great deal of labor. Plashing required constant manipulation of branches and twigs to ensure they grew in the right direction. An improperly planted hedge was virtually impossible to correct. Even after the hedge was established, the farmer had to continually cut back outgrowths.

Another disadvantage was the fact that hedges were nearly immovable. Because the hedge's roots were so firmly entrenched in the ground, attempting to transplant it often damaged the roots enough to kill it. The hedge's thorns, which so effectively deterred cattle, also deterred human hands from reaching its roots. Hedges were also slow to grow, a problem for struggling homesteaders, who needed to establish crops as soon as possible. Furthermore, like wood fences, hedges were susceptible to prairie fires. They were also natural havens for rodents, which devoured not only the hedge's fruit but also nearby crops. Finally, hedges usurped precious water. Thus the best possible fencing solution was still far from a perfect one.

Smooth Wire Fences

Smooth wire fencing was available in the East in the early 1800s, and westerners could buy smooth wire as early as the 1840s. The early wire was not galvanized, so fence builders often painted it to discourage rusting. Through the 1850s and 1860s, manufacturers of smooth wire gradually improved its quality, and by 1870, smooth wire fencing was common.

Smooth wire had several advantages: it was ready for immediate use; it was typically cheaper than other fencing materials sold in the West; it was light and easy to transport; and it was easy to handle. Building a wire fence required far less time and labor than stone walls, soil ridges, furrows, or hedges. By 1870 approximately 350,000 miles of smooth wire was in use by homesteaders in the West.

But smooth wire, like the other fencing options, had its faults. It was particularly ineffective against longhorns, a breed tougher and more aggressive than the breeds of the East, where smooth wire fencing was more effective and therefore more common. Longhorns could bend the wire low enough to trample over it, or they could simply uproot the posts. Moreover, most of the smooth wire manufactured in the 1860s and early 1870s failed to withstand the West's extreme weather. In the winter, the wire became brittle and, in the summer, it tended to droop.

Jacob Haish, the seller of Osage orange seeds, suggested to his customers that entwining the thorny branches of the hedge with smooth wire could deter livestock more effectively. His suggestion hinted at a possible solution to the West's fencing dilemma.

A National Predicament

With each passing year, the fencing problem in the American West grew more obvious and more urgent. The problem was the subject of much discussion in the mid-1800s, perhaps more so than any other issue. The inordinate expense to homesteaders was a key concern. In 1870 one agricultural publication reported that it took an average of $1.74 in fencing to keep livestock from consuming $2.45 worth of crops. Another newspaper of the time noted that the cost to repair the nation's fences was more than the total federal, state, county, and municipal taxes combined.

In the Iowa State Agricultural Society annual report of 1860, the section entitled "What Shall We Do for Fences?" highlighted the precise question that many farmers in the West faced. The report focused on the scarcity of timber in the state and the great expense of rail fences, which severely restricted farmers' profits. The report pointed out the "millions of fruitful acres ready and waiting for the breaking plow" but for the lack of fencing, and concluded that "sometime or other something must be done."

The issue of inadequate fencing was so serious that the federal government studied the situation. The 1871 *Report of the U.S.*

Department of Agriculture confirmed what most western settlers already knew: the cost of fencing in the West made it nearly impracticable to set up farming operations. The study found that it cost a western settler $640 to fence a 160-acre farm, which was between 60 and 300 percent greater than the cost of fencing in other areas of the country. The report attributed the cost to the lack of feasible fencing material in the West. To the delight of many cattlemen and cowboys, many settlers, finding no viable way of farming their land, abandoned their homesteads.

Chapter 5

A Twist of the Wire

Throughout the 1860s and early 1870s, settlers struggled with inadequate fences. But in 1873, more than a decade after the Homestead Act passed, pivotal events were unfolding in a small town approximately sixty miles west of Chicago. The tinkering of several inventors—all from DeKalb, Illinois—would become the beginning of the ultimate solution to the West's fencing dilemma.

Before then, the problem had been wrestled with in numerous ways but never solved. In the first seventy-five years of the nineteenth century, the federal government had issued 1,200 patents for fences of all types, with more than two-thirds of those patents issued after 1865. In a mere three years—from 1866 through 1868—the United States Patent Office issued 365 fence patents. These numbers indicated the country's intense search for a fencing solution for the western frontier. Until one was found, settlement of the West remained largely impractical.

Early Fence Designs

The first known use of barbed metal in fencing occurred in 1857, when John Grinninger, a worker in an Austin, Texas, iron foundry, placed long, narrow pieces of metal with coarse teeth along its edges—and perhaps shards of glass—on the top of a board fence to protect his garden. His neighbors and other Austin citizens, incensed over the cruel nature of his barricade, tried to run him out of town. He refused to leave or to take down his fence enhancement. The controversy ended in 1862, when Grinninger was murdered—although whether the murder was related to his fencing creation remains uncertain.

There is some evidence that from the late 1850s through the 1860s, others in the West had used sharp objects, such as horseshoe nails and spikes, to make fencing more effective. But definitive proof remains lacking because makers of such armored fencing tended not to make their inventions public. Exposing sharp projections to livestock was generally considered cruel, and cattlemen and cowboys were especially disturbed by it.

Though barbed wire inventions were rare outside the United States, two French patents preceded the first American barb patents. In 1860 Leonce Eugene Grassin-Baledans received a patent for a strand of coiled sheet metal fabricated with various pricks and spikes, intended to protect trees. In 1865 Louis François Jannin patented a coiled two-wire strand with diamond-shaped barbs.

Louis François Jannin's two-wire strand, patented June 1865.
—COURTESY OF HAROLD L. HAGEMEIER, FROM
BARBED WIRE IDENTIFICATION ENCYCLOPEDIA

The first patent for an all-metal barb in the United States went to A. T. Kelly of Peoria, Illinois, in 1866. The following year, three U.S. patents are often credited for marking the official appearance of barbed wire on the continent. Alphonso Dabb was granted a patent for a strip of metal affixed with iron spikes, used to prevent people from climbing over fences and walls. The next patent went to Lucien B. Smith for a fence equipped with points, and the last was William D. Hunt's, for a revolving wheel with sharp spurs loosely attached to it.

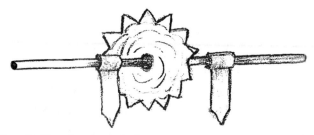

William D. Hunt's wheel design, patent no. 67, 117 (July 23, 1867).
—COURTESY OF HAROLD L. HAGEMEIER, FROM
BARBED WIRE IDENTIFICATION ENCYCLOPEDIA

None of these barbed wire inventions met with significant commercial success, however, perhaps because of poor promotion. Consequently, these inventions would have been unknown to western farming communities such as DeKalb. The ultimate winner of the barbed wire race probably had no way of knowing about these previous designs when he set about devising his own invention in 1873.

"Barb City": DeKalb, Illinois

DeKalb, Illinois, had sprouted up nearly a half century earlier as one of many towns in the upper Mississippi River valley. By the late 1870s, these farming communities had grown into welcome gathering points for covered-wagon travelers, who stopped for rest and supplies before setting off again for the plains farther west. During the 1860s and 1870s, towns such as DeKalb, located along the eastern edge of cattle country, became experimental places for fencing. Almost half of the approximately four hundred fencing designs and fencing tools patented by the end of the nineteenth century were invented by citizens of Illinois. And within that state, a large number of these fencing innovators hailed from one town: DeKalb.

One of these DeKalb inventors was a sixty-year-old farmer named Joseph F. Glidden. Glidden had been raising crops on his six-hundred-acre farm for some time, and like most other farmers on the plains, he understood well the difficulty of keeping livestock out of the crops. In 1873, after three decades of farming, Glidden found the inspiration that would solve the predicament faced by settlers across much of the American West—practical, economical, and effective fencing.

At the county fair that year, Glidden came upon the exhibit of a fellow DeKalb area farmer. Henry M. Rose, from the nearby community of Waterman Station, had on display a simple yet curious design—a strip of wood with nail-like spikes attached to it. Rose's motivation behind making the contraption, which was a fence attachment and not an actual fence, was a desire to control an unruly cow. Glidden and several other men gathered around to study the exhibit. The spiked strip was meant to be attached to a plain wire fence so that the spikes would prick cattle and prevent them from trying to break through.

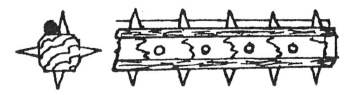

Henry M. Rose's wire design, patent no. 138, 763 (May 13, 1873), which he exhibited at the DeKalb County fair in 1873. —COURTESY OF HAROLD L. HAGEMEIER, FROM *BARBED WIRE IDENTIFICATION ENCYCLOPEDIA*

Glidden's Solution

Joseph Glidden was the man who would ultimately bring the fencing solution to the American West. Urgings from his wife,

Joseph F. Glidden, inventor of the first practical and mass-produced barbed wire design for use in the American West.
—COURTESY OF THE JOSEPH F. GLIDDEN HOMESTEAD & HISTORICAL CENTER

Glidden's barbed wire design, patent no. 157,124 (November 24, 1874), which became known as "The Winner."
—COURTESY OF HAROLD L. HAGEMEIER, FROM *BARBED WIRE IDENTIFICATION ENCYCLOPEDIA*

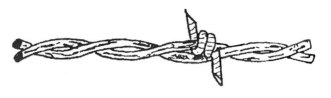

Lucinda, hastened his search for an effective livestock deterrent, for the farm animals constantly invaded her garden. After coming across Henry Rose's exhibit at the county fair, Glidden set to work to improve Rose's wire design. Glidden noticed that the wooden attachment, which slid freely along the smooth wire, could be moved aside by cattle. He believed the barbs could be put to better use if they were attached directly to the fencing material.

Rummaging through his kitchen, Glidden found a coffee mill, and with the help of a blacksmith, he modified the mill so that it twisted short strands of wire into barbs. He intended to slide these barbs onto a wire, but he needed to find a way to keep them

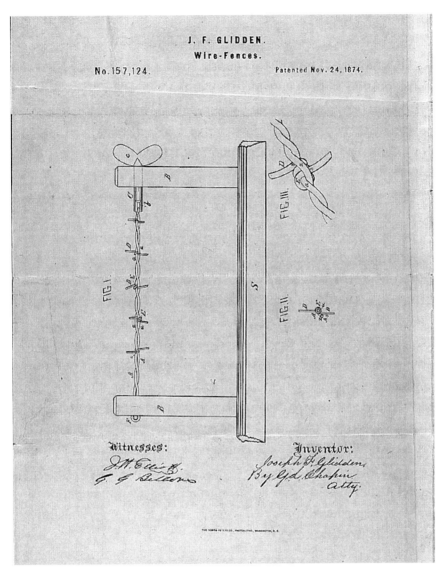

Patent drawing for Joseph F. Glidden's barbed wire design.
His improved design kept the twisted barbs in place and became
the leading barbed wire used in the West. —COURTESY OF
THE NATIONAL ARCHIVES AND RECORDS ADMINISTRATION

from moving freely along the wire. He took the twisted barbs and
looped a long wire strand through them, then intertwined a second wire strand through that. Doing this kept the twisted barbs
in place. Glidden repeated the process until he had made several
hundred feet of the barbed wire. When he finished, he strung his
invention around Lucinda's garden to observe its effect.

When the farm animals approached the fence, they tried to push past the barbed wire into the garden, but when they encountered the barbs, they reared back in pain. Eventually the animals learned to keep away. With a simple twist of the wire, Glidden had come up with a fencing solution for Lucinda—and for farmers across the West.

Barbed wire fencing took less time and labor to construct than limestone walls, dirt ridges, or hedges. It occupied negligible space and cast very little shade. It did not harbor pests or weeds as hedges did. And, most importantly, barbed wire was affordable. The cost and labor were comparable to smooth wire, but barbed wire had none of the disadvantages of its predecessor. The twisted design reinforced the wire's strength, so unlike smooth wire, barbed wire resisted heat in the summer and cold in the winter. And, of course, the barbs discouraged even the most intractable animals—including the tough Texas longhorn.

Although Glidden was not the first inventor of barbed wire, his version was destined to become the most popular fence in the West. Knowing that farmers would be keenly interested in putting this affordable and effective fencing around their crops, Glidden soon turned his attention to his barbed wire's commercial possibilities. He believed that the low production costs of such a simple invention would surely create large profits.

In October 1873, Glidden applied for a patent, the exclusive right to make, use, and sell his invention; he was granted the patent thirteen months later. When he began his operations, Glidden enlisted the help of his wife. Before long, though, he was receiving enough orders to hire someone to help with production. Clearly, the business was headed for success.

The Barb Fence Company

Rose's county fair exhibit had caught the attention of other men besides Glidden. Isaac L. Ellwood, a young hardware store merchant, had also studied the exhibit and engineered his own barbed wire invention, for which he received a patent in February 1874. His design featured a flat-sheet metal ribbon wire with a metal barb. When news about Glidden's barbed wire design spread, Ellwood heard about it. Eager to compare the two inventions, Ellwood and his wife took a ride out to Glidden's farm on an early spring Sunday in 1874.

Much to Ellwood's chagrin, his wife said she thought that Glidden's design was superior to his. Upset at first, Ellwood calmed down and admitted she was right. The following day, Ellwood approached Glidden with a proposition: to become business partners in the manufacture and sale of Glidden's barbed wire.

Although Glidden was interested in the profit-making possibilities of his invention, at age sixty-one he was ready to lighten his business activities. He had already tried to sell his rights to a neighboring farmer, A. Y. Baldwin, for one hundred dollars, but Baldwin had declined, claiming he lacked faith in patents of any kind. So when Ellwood made his offer, Glidden accepted. He felt that Ellwood, still in his forties, would have the requisite energy to drive the business forward.

Glidden sold half of his interest to Ellwood for $265, and the two men became partners, opening for business as the Barb Fence Company. With so many homesteaders in need of feasible fencing material, they were confident that, once the word got around, demand for their barbed wire would explode.

The partners marketed their product through Ellwood's store. They sold approximately 10,000 pounds of barbed wire in their

Isaac L. Ellwood's barbed wire design, patent no. 147,756 (February 24, 1874). —COURTESY OF HAROLD L. HAGEMEIER, FROM *BARBED WIRE IDENTIFICATION ENCYCLOPEDIA*

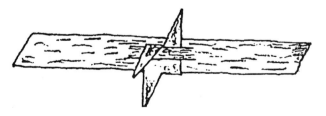

Joseph F. Glidden's house in DeKalb, Illinois, circa 1900.
This was the site where he invented his barbed wire design in 1873.
—COURTESY OF THE JOSEPH F. GLIDDEN HOMESTEAD & HISTORICAL CENTER

first year of operation. In the beginning, they manufactured the product primarily by hand on Glidden's farm in DeKalb. Within a short time, however, they rented a small, inexpensive building. Soon outgrowing that space, they bought a two-story brick building in downtown DeKalb, where they continued to make barbed wire mostly by hand.

Within the first year, demand was so high that the partners turned to machinery for production. In 1875 they constructed a larger building and added a steam engine to power the machines. That year they manufactured and sold more than six hundred thousand pounds of barbed wire—sixty times more than in their first year of operation.

Jacob Haish's "S" Barb

As Glidden and Ellwood were joining forces, another man had also come up with his own barbed wire design. Jacob Haish, a DeKalb lumberman who sold Osage orange seeds to farmers for hedges, had also seen Henry Rose's exhibit at the 1873 county fair, and like

Glidden and Ellwood, he had recognized the potential of barbed fencing. As a grower and seller of hedge seeds for twenty years, he appreciated the difficulties of using hedges as fences and had always been on the lookout for a superior alternative.

Haish submitted a patent application for his barbed wire design in December 1873—two months after Glidden submitted his patent application. Haish received his patent the following month, ten months before Glidden received his. Haish came up with several more designs and applied for patents. In June 1874 he submitted a patent application for his "S" barb design, and he received the patent in August 1875. The "S" barb would become an exceedingly popular barbed wire design in the West, although it would never be as widely used as Glidden's design.

Glidden, Ellwood, and Haish—all from DeKalb—had independently come up with unique barbed wire designs and, within six months of each other, had applied for patents on them. The fact that Haish applied for his first patent after Glidden but received the patent before Glidden would lead to conflicts over the rights to produce and sell barbed wire. But initially the inventors turned their attention to marketing and selling their inventions. No matter whose design emerged on top, the fencing problem that had plagued farmers in the West for decades was finally going to be solved.

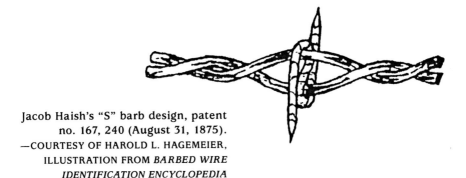

Jacob Haish's "S" barb design, patent
no. 167, 240 (August 31, 1875).
—COURTESY OF HAROLD L. HAGEMEIER,
ILLUSTRATION FROM *BARBED WIRE
IDENTIFICATION ENCYCLOPEDIA*

Chapter 6

Light as Air, Stronger than Whiskey, Cheap as Dirt

Glidden and Ellwood accelerated their manufacturing plans for the Barb Fence Company. Once the company secured the barbed wire market in the vicinity of their hometown of DeKalb, Illinois, it set its sights on Texas, the birthplace of cattle raising. Glidden hoped to bring barbed wire into the heart of cattle country, where farmers were most desperate for fencing. He was also cognizant that a few of the big cattlemen—the cattle barons of the West—were landowners, and he believed they would be just as interested in this new fencing product as farmers.

Glidden sent two salesmen, Henry B. Sanborn and J. P. Warner, to promote the company's barbed wire in Texas. In 1875 the team traveled to Houston. What they found was an unexpected obstacle. A controversy was stirring between cattlemen and settlers over the use of the state's public lands.

For decades, cattle-raising operations had been established throughout the state of Texas, and the industry had grown to have considerable economic power. But by the time Sanborn and Warner went there, the significance of farming to the Texas economy was growing. Nearly all cattlemen insisted on preserving the open range, while farmers continued to divide their parcels up for agriculture, meaning they had a stake in discouraging cattle from tracking through their fields. Adding to the cattlemen's resentment was the fact that many of these homesteads were public lands purchased from the state government, and public lands were supposed to remain open range. As farmers and cattlemen increasingly came into contact with each other, the tension between them was mounting.

Nevertheless, Sanborn and Warner proceeded with their plans to promote Glidden's barbed wire in the Lone Star State. Their attempts netted a few sales, but on the whole, the numbers were disappointing. Perhaps not surprisingly, cattlemen poked fun at the idea that little bits of wire could hold back cattle, especially longhorns. More perplexing was the fact that the farmers–the very people whom Glidden had in mind when he invented the product—were skeptical. As much as they needed an economical solution to their fencing problems, they, too, doubted that strands of wire could repel unruly livestock. Merchants also resisted, doubtful that their customers would purchase the untested product. In the end, the Texas trip was a big disappointment for the Barb Fence Company.

Military Plaza Demonstration

In spite of the setback, Glidden wasn't ready to give up on Texas. As Glidden was pondering his next move, John Warne Gates, a young Illinois hardware salesman with a penchant for risky ventures, entered the picture. "Bet-a-Million" Gates, as he was later called, was aggressive, persistent, and domineering, all characteristics necessary to relate successfully to Texans. In 1876, having heard about this fencing innovation and immediately seeing its potential, Gates met with Glidden and Ellwood to discuss taking a crack at the task that Sanborn and Warner had failed at. Glidden and Ellwood agreed to hire Gates as their new Texas barbed wire salesman.

Gates went straight to the heart of cattle country—San Antonio—to get to know his potential customers. San Antonio was a thriving town where cattlemen and cowboys congregated

John W. "Bet-a-Million" Gates.
—COURTESY OF THE MUSEUM OF THE GULF COAST, PORT ARTHUR, TEXAS

and conducted business in post–Civil War times. Gates arrived on the scene in 1876 with little more than a charming smile, a clever mind, and a belief in the effectiveness of his product.

Precisely how Gates opened up the Texas market remains disputed, but many sources agree that he caught people's attention with the boast that Glidden's barbed wire was "light as air, stronger than whiskey, cheap as dirt." By day, Gates talked to farmers in Military Plaza, a gathering place where vendors sold their wares and residents shopped and socialized. At night he mingled with cattlemen in the nearby casino. He was exceptionally sociable and likeable, and it wasn't long before he had befriended numerous prospective customers.

As the story goes, Gates then devised an unusual demonstration. He began constructing something in Military Plaza, and onlookers began to gather and watch as it took shape. Refusing to reveal his intentions, Gates let murmurs about his mysterious contraption spread through the town. After a while it became apparent that he was building a corral using barbed wire, the

46

Military Plaza in San Antonio, Texas, the site where John W. Gates performed his barbed wire corral demonstration. —USED WITH PERMISSION OF DOCUMENTING THE AMERICAN SOUTH, THE UNIVERSITY OF NORTH CAROLINA AT CHAPEL HILL LIBRARIES

newfangled invention he'd been going on about. Having piqued the interest of most of the population of San Antonio, Gates loudly challenged the local cattlemen to "get the wildest damn cattle in Texas—corral 'em here with barbed wire and then let 'em try to get out."

As cattlemen, cowboys, and farmers gathered around Military Plaza, Gates took bets on whether the belligerent longhorns could break through his enclosure. The crowd grew larger as more bets poured in and the excitement built.

In a dramatic display, Gates released the herd into the barbed wire corral. The lean and testy longhorns thundered in and immediately sped toward the fence, intent on bullying their way past it. As they made contact with the barbed wire, they drew back in pain. Enraged, they again charged the fence and again recoiled in pain. The herd continued on in this way, repeatedly challenging the integrity of the barbed wire fence while the fence continued to hold. Finally, the herd settled down with no more interest in breaking their boundaries. Barbed wire had won out against the toughest breed of cattle in the West.

Soon Gates was inundated with orders from people who had seen or heard about the demonstration. Barbed wire was off and running.

The Race to Produce Barbed Wire

News of the amazing new fencing material barreled across Texas and over the windswept plains, prairies, and ranges of the West. In 1874, the first year of the Barb Fence Company's production and two years before Gates's trip to San Antonio, the company had earned a modest profit, hand-producing and selling ten thousand pounds of barbed wire. By 1876, the year of Gates's triumph at Military Plaza, the company's sales had jumped to 2.84 million pounds—with no end in sight.

From the beginning of their business partnership, however, Glidden and Ellwood had had to deal with competition. Jacob Haish, the DeKalb man who had come up with the "S" barb, set about creating his own barbed wire empire. Haish claimed that he, not Glidden, was the inventor of barbed wire. Glidden had applied for his barbed wire patent in October 1873. Even though Haish did not file the application for his first barb design until December 1873, about two months after Glidden's application, Haish received his patent approval first. He felt so strongly about his right to the invention that he placed his claim on the doorway of his residence: "Jacob Haish, Inventor of Barbed Wire."

Glidden, Ellwood, and Haish weren't the only ones jumping into the barbed wire business. Washburn & Moen Manufacturing Company in Massachusetts—the nation's largest manufacturer of smooth wire—took careful note of the happenings. The sudden

Washburn & Moen's wire exhibit (1876). For a time, the company was the nation's largest wire manufacturer.
—PRINT AND PICTURE COLLECTION, THE FREE LIBRARY OF PHILADELPHIA

increase in demand for the company's smooth wire, which the inventors were buying to make their barbed wire, warranted their attention.

The vice president of Washburn & Moen, Charles F. Washburn, traveled to DeKalb in 1876 to seek out the men who were dabbling in wire fencing. Washburn first approached Jacob Haish with an offer to purchase an interest in his barbed wire business. Appalled by Haish's exceedingly high asking price of $200,000— equivalent to almost $4 million in today's terms—Washburn refused. Washburn then went to Glidden to see about joining the Barb Fence Company's endeavor, and Glidden readily accepted an offer. In May 1876, Glidden sold his 50 percent interest in the barbed wire patent to the country's largest manufacturer of smooth wire for $60,000 plus royalty rights. Ellwood retained part ownership in the company. The Barb Fence Company became I. L. Ellwood & Company of DeKalb.

With the capital and technology that Washburn's company provided, serious production of barbed wire accelerated to meet the growing demand. In 1876 I. L. Ellwood & Company began production in its Worcester, Massachusetts, location. The Worcester branch took responsibility for supplying the southern and southwestern states, while Ellwood retained the western states as his territory.

In 1877 the nation's total production of barbed wire was nearly thirteen million pounds. The following year, production doubled, to over twenty-six million pounds. And in 1879 production nearly doubled again, to more than fifty million pounds. And so it went year after year. I. L. Ellwood & Company produced the bulk of the barbed wire—over eighty million pounds in 1880. But as barbed wire sales continued to skyrocket, trouble began to brew.

An advertisement by I. L. Ellwood & Co. portraying the Glidden barb fence as an impervious barrier, one that animals of all sorts will not jump. —COURTESY OF THE ELLWOOD HOUSE ASSOCIATION

Chapter 7

The Devil's Rope

ettlers in the West eagerly embraced barbed wire. With its prickly barbs, they were able to protect their crop fields, and its affordability and ease of use enabled them to improve their homesteads quickly and cheaply. But along with the rise of barbed wire's popularity arose plenty of discontent. The established inhabitants of the West—cattlemen, cowboys, and Native Americans—were not happy about the new fences, which interfered with their ability to freely traverse the land as they had in the past.

Fencing Out Native Culture

By the time barbed wire was invented, many Native Americans had already been displaced from their traditional lands by white settlement and relocated to reservations by concerted federal force. But some Plains Indians still roamed the open range—primarily in Texas, Indian Territory (Oklahoma), Nebraska, and Kansas. As barbed wire went up across the land, these tribes found themselves increasingly fenced off and unable to move freely, inhibiting their ability to follow and hunt the buffalo and other animals they relied on for food. Barbed wire was such a severe threat to their traditional way of life that some Indians called it "the devil's rope."

A herd of American buffalo feeding on the grasses in Black Hills, South Dakota (circa 1960). As late as 1865, the species still numbered around fifteen million. By 1883 it was close to extinction and numbered fewer than 300. Today, the American buffalo population is approximately 4,000. —FRED HULTSTRAND HISTORY IN PICTURES COLLECTION, NDIRS-NDSU, FARGO

Barbed wire not only interfered with the Indians' movement but also impeded the movement of the animals. As effective at repelling buffalo as it was cattle, the devil's rope interrupted the natural grazing patterns of buffalo. As a result, they overgrazed much pastureland. In these overtaxed areas, grass wilted and herds ran out of food. Buffalo populations decreased. Thus barbed wire intensified an already grave downward spiral for both the buffalo and the Native Americans who depended on them.

A Threat to the Open Range

While the Indians suffered from the increasingly widespread use of barbed wire, the most significant antagonism towards the innovation came from cattlemen and cowboys. Barbed wire posed a direct threat to the open range, and therefore to their livelihoods. Cattle owners depended on access to public land for grazing and watering areas, and barbed wire fences impeded that access, driving up the costs of already expensive cattle-raising operations.

The seriousness of the problem became most evident during the seasonal trail drives, the transport of cattle to market. The physical barriers interfered greatly with the drives to the transport stations in Kansas and Missouri. In time, some cattlemen dropped out of the business altogether. All during the 1870s, the number of cattle driven each year steadily decreased. By 1880 many cattle drivers and cowboys were unemployed.

Further Anti–Barbed Wire Sentiment

Indians and cattle folk weren't the only ones complaining about barbed wire. Many farmers and townspeople protested that the use of sharp barbs was inhumane. Cattle suffered and sometimes died from wounds caused by barbed wire. Even lingering close to barbed wire could endanger cattle: lightning sometimes struck the wire fencing and killed livestock grazing nearby.

Eventually, anti–barbed wire groups formed to combat the use of the devil's rope and to persuade legislators to make individuals who erected fences responsible for the damage they caused to livestock. Different western states took different approaches to the problem. A few proposed an outright ban on barbed wire fences. For example, a bill banning the fences was introduced in the Texas legislature in 1879, though it ultimately failed to pass. Even in Illinois, Glidden's home state, the legislature did not formally legalize the use of barbed wire fences until 1887, fourteen years after Glidden created his design.

Even in the East, where farmers held more power than in the West and where barbed wire was less common, some legislators were concerned about the damage caused by the material. In 1879 and 1880, bills prohibiting barbed wire fences were brought before the legislatures of Connecticut, Vermont, New Hampshire, and Maine.

Sometimes compromises were hammered out. In states permitting the use of barbed wire fences, some courts held fence owners responsible for damages the fences caused unless they were constructed in a way that protected or warned cattle. In Texas, for instance, though the ban on barbed wire failed, the legislature did for a time impose a requirement that barbed wire fences have a board placed between the top strands to give livestock warning. In Nebraska, an 1881 statute made it unlawful to put up a barbed wire fence "without first putting up sufficient guards to prevent either man or beast from running into said fence."

Many of the longstanding inhabitants of the West, frustrated by the growing use of barbed wire, directed their hostility toward the settlers themselves. But they also feared their growing power.

Chapter 8

The Fence Cutting Wars

W ithin a few years of homesteaders' embrace of barbed wire, tensions surrounding the use of the fences escalated from hostility and threats to outright property destruction and physical attacks. The stage was set for a full-scale battle between the users and the opponents of barbed wire fences.

The new fencing material had had a profound effect on western settlement. Many Americans who had previously chosen not to go West because of the fencing problem changed their minds when they learned about barbed wire. In 1870 the nation's farms had numbered approximately 2.7 million; by 1880 that number had increased to approximately 4 million, with most of the increase attributed to the agricultural settlement of the American West. In eleven western states alone, the number of farms increased nearly 74 percent in the 1870s.

Cattlemen Take a Stand

As the newcomers flooded into their territory, cattlemen dug in their heels. They and their livestock had been roaming the open range long before government-supported settlement had begun in the West. They believed they had as much right to the land as anyone else—and according to the tradition of the open range, that right was being violated. They were not about to give up the

West without a fight. At first, cattlemen and other barbed wire opponents focused their efforts on illegal fencing.

The practice of claiming and fencing land illegally was one of the most alarming byproducts of western settlement. While most settlers filed their claims and improved their homesteads legally, some put barbed wire fences around land not their own, obstructing access to what was open public land. Many of these land-grabbers were settlers who wanted more land than the Homestead Act provided. Especially in Texas, settlers came in and unlawfully enclosed public property with barbed wire fences, presumably hoping to file claims, lease, or buy the land later. By physically taking control of a parcel, they discouraged law-abiding settlers from trying to claim the land under the Homestead Act.

Fed up, cattlemen and other barbed wire opponents in the West, especially in Colorado, Texas, and the territories of New Mexico and Wyoming, filed land-use petitions and formal grievances to local authorities. More often than not, however, they met with little success. Some authorities were slow to investigate the grievances, and even those who did order the squatters to vacate the land and take down the fencing usually did little to enforce the orders.

Fence Cutting

When it became apparent that pleas to authorities regarding illegal claims produced little action, cattlemen took matters into their own hands. Desperate to protect their way of life, they began cutting down barbed wire fences. At first they cut only illegal fences, but the cutting soon spread to lawful ones, including those on homestead claims. Wielding a pair of wire cutters, these cowboys and cattlemen cut down any fences that blocked passage to water sources or grazing areas. Fence cutters were difficult to catch because they often worked at night and usually wore masks or bandannas.

The general public—largely made up of other cattlemen and cowboys—overwhelmingly opposed fencing and refused to turn in the fence cutters. They viewed the practice as civil disobedience committed by honest citizens trying to secure their livelihood and preserve the open range tradition. So even when fence cutters were caught, authorities found it hard to convict them, for local juries were loathe to find them guilty.

Once the fence cutters began attacking fences around legitimate homesteads, matters quickly spiraled out of control. Settlers and other landowners were just as determined to protect their own livelihood. Having little other recourse, many land-owners who had been attacked by fence cutters simply erected new fences. Those who could spare the time sometimes patrolled their fences, often taking their six-shooters along.

Fence cutting soon became widespread in the American West, affecting states and territories as far east as Kansas and as far north as Montana. The fence cutting wars broke out in full

Masked fence cutters in Custer County, Nebraska. This photo is a re-enactment of the 1885 fence cutting of barbed wire on the Brighton Ranch. —NEBRASKA STATE HISTORICAL SOCIETY (IMAGE ID NBHIPS 12299)

force in Texas in 1881. The conflict quickly spread across the state to the western edges of the frontier, then north to Colorado and Wyoming and Montana Territories.

As the struggle between fence cutters and fence builders escalated, outlaws seized the opportunity to profit from the turmoil. Cattle rustlers—thieves who stole unbranded calves or altered brands of branded cattle—took advantage of the fence cutting chaos to seize cattle and land. Many of these criminals pretended to side with the cattlemen, but in reality they were more interested in perpetuating the disorder for their own interests. Outlaws, including some disgruntled cattlemen, organized into fence cutting gangs. Brandishing six-shooters, they often threatened or attacked people who challenged them.

The line between cattlemen cutting fences to drive their cattle and outlaws deliberately creating chaos in order to commit crimes became blurred. The thieves took what they wanted as long as they believed they could get away with it. No westerner was safe from attack.

Fight or Flight

Many settlers and other landowners attacked by fence cutters continued to rebuild their fences. Often the new fences would immediately be cut down again. Some fence cutters not only cut the new fence but also dug up and dragged away the fence posts. In some areas, fence cutting gangs posted messages such as "Let your wire stay down" and "We will cut it as fast as you can build it." In many cases, the signs were enough to keep the owner from rebuilding. Some gangs were known to steal property, burn fields and homes, and even poison water sources.

It did not take long before fence cutters and homesteaders began shooting at each other. Although no records clearly document the exact number of murders in the West, violence was an accepted part of western life. Defending one's rights with firearms, on whichever side, was a respected rule of conduct. In

Texas, where the fence cutting wars originated, two fence-related murders were confirmed.

The fence cutting wars climaxed in 1883. In Texas alone, more than half of the counties reported fence cutting. Amid the general disorder, many businessmen on both sides stalled their operations due to the threat of violence. Much to the satisfaction of many cattlemen and cowboys, some settlers fled the West in the early 1880s, abandoning their homestead claims and their fences.

Land Value

Personal injury and property destruction were not the only damages resulting from the fence cutting wars. Without the ability of settlers to farm in peace, land quickly lost value. In Texas, for instance, property damage amounted to $20 million during the fence cutting wars, and land value decreased by as much as $30 million. Some companies that had speculated in land in the West sought to unload their holdings, which only exacerbated the decline.

The loss in land value had immediate repercussions. First, it discouraged many would-be settlers from going West. It also discouraged many existing landowners from making improvements and repairs on their land. Banks became unwilling to take land as collateral for loans, leaving many landowners in financial straits. As ever-larger numbers of settlers gave up and abandoned their plots, land values plummeted even further.

Finally, settlers caught up in the chaos received some relief when federal and state authorities came to their aid. Despite overwhelming public support for the cattlemen, authorities made a deliberate decision to defy the longstanding Law of the Open Range.

The Government Steps In

Texas, where fence cutting wars had begun, was the first state to act decisively to stop the violence. During the late 1870s and into the early 1880s, the Texas legislature was deluged with letters protesting the lawlessness overcoming the land and petitioning for the state's intervention. Unlike other states and territories at the time, Texas was still managing its own public lands.

In 1883 Texas governor John Ireland visited the counties where fence cutting had become particularly destructive, many north of Dallas near the Texas–Indian Territory line. Later that year, Ireland called for a special legislative session to find ways to end the violence. After much debate, including a proposal to simply allow the killing of any individual caught in the act of cutting fences, the final law, passed by the Texas legislature in February 1884, made the act of fence cutting a felony punishable by one to five years in jail. The act of erecting illegal fences was deemed a misdemeanor. As a concession to cattlemen, the law also deemed that all public roads be kept open and that fence builders install a gate every one-third mile in fences that touched on public roads. This requirement allowed cowboys to move herds through and retain access to public grazing areas.

To uphold these laws, the state government called upon the Texas Rangers to police known danger areas of the state. The Texas Rangers, originally a militia organized in 1823 to police the frontier, had by then evolved into an official law enforcement agency. Its role in upholding the new fence cutting law would be crucial.

Ultimately, the Texas Rangers helped restore order in areas where the fence cutting wars had been most deeply felt. Although incidents of fence cutting occasionally marred the Texas landscape in the years that followed, the 1884 law, combined with the Rangers' diligent enforcement, successfully quelled the upheaval.

Starting in 1885, the federal government also began enforcing laws against fence cutting violence. With its stated policy of promoting western settlement, the U.S. government was a natural ally of homesteaders in the fight for barbed wire. It also had a financial incentive to push for barbed wire's acceptance. Many cattlemen instructed their cowboys to drive livestock back and forth from one county to the next to confuse tax collectors. Adequate fencing would allow the government to collect more taxes more easily.

By 1885, the fence cutting wars were largely quieted, bringing the federal government one step closer to creating the agricultural nation it desired. But as settlement of the West grew denser and barbed wire crossed more and more of the formerly open range, conflicts over barbed wire fences would persist. Illegal fence building would become more common than fence cutting as barbed wire continued to work its way across the West.

Chapter 9
Moonshine Wire

While cattlemen and settlers battled it out in the fence cutting wars of the West, a legal battle in the East had been preoccupying the barbed wire industry from the mid-1870s to the early 1880s. The main opponents were barbed wire patent holders versus those who were manufacturing and selling barbed wire without rights to the patents.

Trying to gain control over the barbed wire market, I. L. Ellwood & Company had been buying up rights to many barbed wire–related patents. The company also purchased patent rights to several machines used to make the wire. Others who were or wanted to be in the barbed wire game were troubled by the company's potential monopoly.

Jacob Haish was the first to stir up trouble for I. L. Ellwood & Company. Soon after receiving the patent for his first barbed wire design in 1874, Haish had filed interference papers against Glidden. From that point on, Haish made the public aware of his claims and counterclaims using billboards, newspaper and magazine advertisements, and other vehicles. Glidden and later I. L. Ellwood & Company feuded with Haish for years over who had the right to manufacture and sell barbed wire. Haish continually filed various lawsuits against his rivals, remaining adamant that,

Portrait of Jacob Haish.
—COURTESY OF JEFF J. MARSHALL
(www.JacobHaishMfg.org)

because his patent had been approved before Glidden's, he was the true inventor of barbed wire.

A Growing Industry

As the barbed wire market exploded into a multimillion dollar industry, inventors across the country created and patented hundreds of barbed wire designs. The flurry of inventions and designs resulted in more than 570 barbed wire patents and 2,000 other patents related to barbed wire. And because barbed wire was relatively cheap and easy to produce, people with no previous experience making wire or fences—blacksmiths, carpenters, mechanics—jumped into manufacturing the product.

Small factories took root all over Missouri, Iowa, Illinois, and Kansas, as well as in the East. In Illinois alone, twenty-nine factories were producing barbed wire. At an average cost of $150 per mile, barbed wire fencing in the 1870s was only half the cost of board and picket fences. As inventors developed more efficient machines, barbed wire became even cheaper to produce, which led to still lower prices.

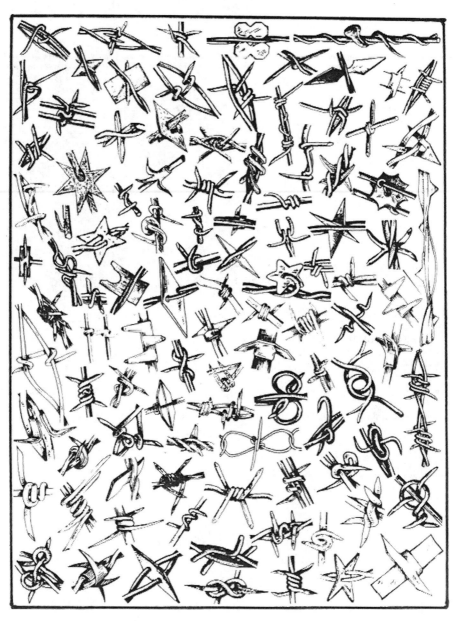

Collage of barbed wire designs. The demand for barbed wire in the West spawned the creation of numerous designs. —COURTESY OF THE HISTORICAL MUSEUM OF BARB WIRE AND FENCING TOOLS, AKA DEVIL'S ROPE MUSEUM

With the introduction of cheap, effective fences, more and more settlers applied for homestead grants, and the population of the West steadily increased. The government's vision of turning wilderness into farmland was becoming a reality. As the frontier grew more densely settled, good 160-acre plots became harder to find, so smaller farms soon appeared. Smaller farms meant more enclosures, which meant more sales of barbed wire fencing.

Barbed wire sales agents traveled door-to-door throughout the West. As settlers bought up the wire for their farms, the industry accelerated, energizing the economy and spilling money into the pockets of the manufacturers and salesmen, as well as those of the businesses that served them.

The demand for barbed wire put men to work. This group of men worked in Jacob Haish's barbed wire factory in DeKalb, Illinois, in 1910.
—COURTESY OF THE JOINER HISTORY ROOM, SYCAMORE, IL

Patent Violators

So eager were businesspeople to get a piece of the growing barbed wire pie that many manufactured it illegally rather than purchasing the licenses to produce and sell the patented wire. Some chose to duplicate and sell Glidden's design, while others produced and sold other inventors' patented designs.

Perhaps the most notable patent violation involved John "Bet-a-Million" Gates, the charismatic salesman who had launched Glidden's product in Texas. By 1877 Gates was looking for more compensation from the company. He wanted to receive a larger percentage of profits, acquire exclusive rights to sales in Texas, or become a partner in the company. Ellwood and Washburn refused his demands, so Gates resigned and set out to make his own mark in the industry.

In 1877 Gates started his own business, the Southern Wire Company, which manufactured illegal wire. He started off with a modest operation, but it grew quickly and reaped big profits. Gates did not lack customers—he had retained many from his Texas days and had won over many new ones in St. Louis and elsewhere. As his company flourished, he repeatedly merged his business with others, each time increasing his stake in the barbed wire business. Eventually his company became the largest manufacturer and distributor of illegal barbed wire.

Others who ran unlicensed barbed wire businesses looked to Gates as a kind of heroic David standing up to Washburn and Ellwood's Goliath. Gates and others producing barbed wire illegally became known as "moonshiners," in reference to moonshine liquor, which, like the wire, was illegally produced. Like distillers of moonshine liquor, barbed wire moonshiners worked under discreet conditions, often at night, and away from the watchful eyes of authorities. Barbed wire moonshiners paid no royalty fees to the patent owner, giving them considerably lower production costs. They easily slashed prices, underselling legitimate manufacturers and upsetting the barbed wire market. By disregarding the rules, patent violators incited general confusion in the industry and threatened the stability of the U.S. patent system.

Washburn and Ellwood actively tried to stem the tide of violations, and they managed to close down 139 factories. During the early 1880s, fifty-three cases were tried against illegal manufacturers in five states—Iowa, Missouri, Kansas, Minnesota, and Nebraska. Farmers across the West anxiously followed the legal disputes and contemplated the impact of this issue on their ability to purchase barbed wire. The tension heightened.

Troubled Purchasers

Moonshiners were not the only ones under scrutiny. The purchasers of moonshine wire—farmers, settlers, and merchants—grew uneasy, and rightfully so. According to the law, the buyer or user could be held equally responsible for violating patent rights, whether or not he was aware of the product's status. Many buyers found their actions monitored by licensed manufacturers and dealers.

As a result, many farmers treated all barbed wire sellers—including bona fide ones—with suspicion. Some companies promised to defend any suits against their customers. Their hope of dispelling fears with this guarantee, however, proved ineffective. Meanwhile, in some areas worried farmers chose to take proactive measures, organizing protective societies to defend any member who came under legal attack.

The Free Wire Movement

In the barbed wire patent controversy, people began to take sides. Many felt that the patent violations were justified to combat Washburn and Ellwood's virtual monopoly. Those in favor of this particular civil disobedience, including moonshiners and some farmers and other landowners, became known as "free wire" supporters. Rallying behind Haish and Gates, they advocated settlers' use of unlicensed wire fencing.

Moonshiners' reasons for favoring free wire were obviously mostly mercenary, but others supported the movement on principle. To many, Washburn and Ellwood's monopoly had the potential to wreak havoc on the barbed wire market and the overall economy. Soon, many legitimate manufacturers of lesser-known barbed wire designs also allied with the moonshiners to resist Washburn and Ellwood.

Politics played no small part in the free wire movement. Many free wire boosters were prominent men, wealthy and politically influential. Other proponents were politicians, seizing the opportunity to win the votes of farmers who faulted the patent system for the barbed wire mess. These politicians introduced legislative measures against the patent system, hoping to allow more wire producers into the market, thus lowering the price of barbed wire.

In Iowa, support for free wire was so strong that the state legislature passed a resolution requesting that the attorney general bring suit against Washburn and Ellwood's barbed wire trust. Although ultimately unsuccessful, Iowa did manage to appropriate $5,000 in federal aid for farmers fighting the barbed wire monopoly.

Inventors Defend the Patent System

Inventors across the country were dismayed as the popularity of the free wire movement grew and patent violators operated their illegal businesses with increasing impunity. At a national convention of inventors, delegates tried to concoct ways to halt the attack on the patent system and stave off its complete breakdown. The crisis required urgent action.

In 1879—the same year Thomas Edison demonstrated his famous electric lamp—Edison threw his influence into the barbed wire frenzy. Urged on by pleas from fellow inventors, Edison summoned Congress's intervention to protect patent rights: "I have spoken of myself and my inventions only in order to protect in the interest of all other inventors against any legislation calculated

Thomas Edison, inventor of the incandescent electric light and holder of more than a thousand patents. Edison used his influence to help put an end to barbed wire patent violations. —COURTESY OF DENVER PUBLIC LIBRARY, HARRY M. RHOADS, WESTERN HISTORY COLLECTION, RH-863

to make our traditional struggle against the capitalists any more difficult." Edison's concern gained public attention and ultimately helped convince Congress to take action against the violations.

I. L. Ellwood & Company Triumph

Through the end of the 1870s and into most of 1880, Ellwood and Washburn continued to fight against the numerous infringements on their patent rights. They wrote to the alleged infringers, demanding that they cease their actions. They also addressed various pleas to the public, hoping to sway opinion.

In addition, Ellwood and Washburn hired people to visit barbed wire dealers and show them how to identify the company's designs. Washburn himself traveled west to try to persuade patent violators to see his position. He also sent out a series of pamphlets to explain patent violations to dealers and buyers of moonshine wire.

The definitive blow to barbed wire patent violators arrived in 1880, when the judgment came down in *Washburn & Moen Manufacturing Co. v. Haish*. By this time, Glidden's barbed wire was the best-selling design in the West, although in Iowa, Haish's "S" barb was perhaps equally popular. On December 15, 1880, a court decision declared Haish in violation of Glidden's patent as well as of several other foundation patents owned by the company. The decision rendered Haish liable for damages accrued. According to the judgment, the profits Haish had earned from his wire since 1874 were not rightfully his but I. L. Ellwood & Company's because the latter had the sole and exclusive right to produce barbed wire.

The immediate effect of the ruling was disastrous for moonshiners and other free wire supporters. It essentially made all independent manufacturers who had violated I. L. Ellwood & Company's patents liable to the company for back royalties. Thirty-three companies were deemed illegal manufacturers and were assessed back damages. Many of these operations went out of business. Those that remained financially viable had to make a decision: apply for licenses to manufacture under the foundation patents owned by Washburn and Ellwood, or abandon the business.

The final death knell to illegal manufacturers and the free wire movement sounded in July 1881, when Haish signed an agreement with I. L. Ellwood & Company assigning it his rights to the "S" barb and other patents. In return, he was granted a license to manufacture and sell barbed wire, with royalty payments to be paid to the company. When free wire supporters discovered the deal Haish had struck, they were left without a leader, and the movement quickly died out.

Over a decade later, in 1892, the U.S. Supreme Court finally heard the last of Haish's and Glidden's many lawsuits, *Washburn & Moen Manufacturing Co. et al. v. Beat 'Em All Barbed-Wire Company*. By then, the question of who had won the barbed wire patent battle had already been settled. In this judgment, the court conceded that Glidden may not have been the true originator of the barbed wire concept, but that there was nonetheless no doubt that he was the first one to patent the barbed wire design. There was also no doubt that Glidden was the first to make the wire widely available to the public. It was Glidden's wire, the court declared, that "spread until there is scarcely a cattle-raising district in the world in which it is not extensively employed." On that basis, Glidden's barbed wire patent was declared "the Winner," and Glidden was awarded the title "the Father of Barbed Wire." The patent battle over barbed wire was finally over.

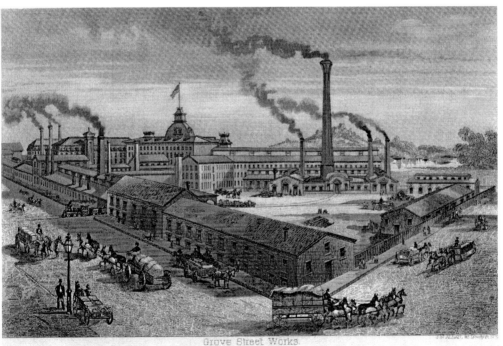

Illustration of Washburn & Moen Manufacturing Co. building in Worcester, Massachusetts (before 1900). —CREATED BY J. W. ALLEN; COURTESY OF WORCESTER PUBLIC LIBRARY

Chapter 10
Full Steam Ahead

During the last three decades of the nineteenth century, growing lines of barbed wire fences were not the only thing altering the landscape of the American West. After the completion of the transcontinental railroad in 1869, train tracks soon crisscrossed what had only recently been open range. The railroad would present challenges for the cattle industry. Like barbed wire, the railways were strangling the open range. At the same time, however, the railroad created new opportunities and opened new markets for cattlemen. In the end, for better or worse, they had no choice but to adapt.

The railroads represented not only a new way of doing business for cattlemen, but also a new market for the barbed wire industry. As westerners discovered that train tracks were a hazard for livestock, they demanded that the railroads fence off their right-of-ways, creating a bonanza for I. L. Ellwood & Company and other barbed wire manufacturers.

For the railroad companies, some of these outcomes had been foreseen, some not. Their goal of extending their lines to the farthest corners of the American West, however, had been in the works for decades. And by the early 1860s, the government was ready to help.

The Pacific Railway Act

In 1862, the same year Congress passed the Homestead Act, Congress also passed the Pacific Railway Act, which helped fund the construction of a railway from the Missouri River to the Pacific Ocean. The plan would expand existing rail lines in the East and Midwest all the way to the West Coast, creating a transcontinental railroad. The act expressed the government's commitment to railways, which it foresaw as a major contributor to settling the West.

The Pacific Railway Act gave two railroads—the Union Pacific Railroad Company and the Central Pacific Railroad Company—the right-of-way on applicable public lands and lent them hundreds of millions of dollars to construct the railroad, which was to run roughly along the thirty-second parallel. In 1863, the Union Pacific began construction in Omaha, Nebraska, and moved westward, while the Central Pacific began at the other end of the route,

One of the first businesses that settlers established in new railroad towns were general stores such as the one pictured here (likely in North Dakota, early 1900s).
—FRED HULTSTRAND HISTORY IN PICTURES COLLECTION, NDIRS-NDSU, FARGO

in Sacramento, California, and moved eastward. After serious delays, most notably the Civil War, the two companies' tracks finally joined at Promontory, Utah, in 1869. The cost of the railroad was $50 million, a huge sum in those days.

As part of the original act, Congress also gave the railroad companies millions of acres of western land, which the railroad companies could later sell to repay their loans. This would benefit the government not only by getting its money back, but also by encouraging settlement. At the same time, the railroad companies benefited from encouraging settlement because it created new customers for them. The railroads actively advertised for settlers to establish homes and towns near new and upcoming rail lines, all with the intent to increase the demand for goods to be shipped

An 1872 advertisement by the Burlington & Missouri River Railroad Company to induce people to settle in Iowa and Nebraska. —LIBRARY OF CONGRESS, RARE BOOK AND SPECIAL COLLECTIONS DIVISION

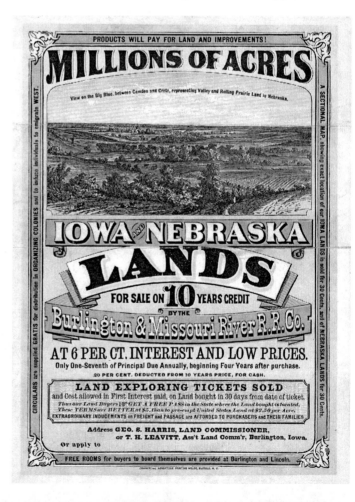

on their railways. Across the West, the railroad companies created towns out of nothing, sometimes in a matter of weeks.

Fencing the Tracks

The transcontinental railroad was considered a monumental achievement. But as the railroads expanded their reach into the West, they confronted a difficulty that only barbed wire could solve. The train tracks often ran through areas where settlers and cattlemen had roaming stock. All types of domestic animals wandered onto the railways, especially in bad weather, and many of these animals met untimely deaths when trains struck them. Over time, such livestock losses mounted until they became a significant financial hardship for stock owners.

Both cattlemen and farmers united on this issue of livestock losses due to unfenced railways. The railroad companies, too, were concerned. Livestock on the railways presented a threat of derailment and injury to passengers. Moreover, the railroad companies were sometimes responsible for paying damages to the owners of the animals killed by their trains.

Most state legislatures agreed that it made more sense to place the responsibility for fencing on the railroad companies than to require thousands of individual livestock owners to build fences to keep their animals away from the tracks. Because livestock losses were higher in the more populated western states, such as Missouri and Kansas, the legislatures of these states were among the first to pass laws requiring railroad companies to fence off their right-of-ways—Missouri in 1865, and Kansas and Minnesota in 1874.

In the 1880s and 1890s, as settlers moved farther west, more and more states enacted laws making railroad companies fence their tracks. Some states also required that the fences have openings every mile or so to allow settlers and cattlemen to lead their livestock through areas that had become congested with barbed wire. Texas was the first to do so, in 1887; similar laws were passed in Montana and Colorado in 1891, and in Nebraska in 1895.

At first, railroad companies needing to build fences faced the same dilemma as settlers did. Fencing material in the 1860s and early 1870s was in scarce supply, and no matter what material was used, enclosing thousands of miles of right-of-ways would be an enormous expense in material and labor. Through the mid-1870s, the railroads used wood for fences, but in the long run this proved impracticable. For one thing, there was little wood to be found on the plains, so it had to be brought in. The farther west the tracks extended, the greater the cost of transporting the heavy wooden boards. Not only was the initial cost of material and labor exorbitant, but the upkeep was costly as well. Wood was a valuable commodity in the West, and board fences out on the prairie were occasionally pilfered by homesteaders. Sometimes railroad employees went out to repair fences only to find nothing left to repair. It is no surprise, then, that railroad companies were among the first to embrace barbed wire.

From the beginning of his involvement with the barbed wire business, Isaac L. Ellwood had diligently pursued railroad companies as potential customers. Ellwood convinced the railroads to try this new invention in 1877. He allowed the companies to try a test run before they paid for it, and the gamble paid off. Railroads quickly began buying barbed wire to fence up all the right-of-ways in the West. By 1879 Ellwood was providing barbed wire to fifty-nine railroad companies; by 1885 he was selling to over one hundred of them.

In 1881—the same year the fence cutting wars broke out—U.S. railways covered nearly 94,000 miles, much of which required fencing on both sides of the tracks. Other barbed wire makers—including Jacob Haish with his "S" barb wire—also rushed to meet railroad companies' demand. Railroad companies became one of the chief consumers of barbed wire in the 1880s and 1890s.

As railroads enclosed their tracks within barbed wire barriers, another conflict emerged. Some farmers and cattlemen removed the fences from the right-of-ways and dragged them away for their own use, just as they had done previously with the wood rail fences. To combat the problem, barbed wire manufacturers created unique variations of Glidden's two-point wire design for the railroads' exclusive use. Any cattleman or farmer found with the railroads' wire design could easily be identified as a wire thief.

The Railroad in Cattle Country

It did not take much time for railroad executives to recognize the windfall their companies might see if cattlemen began to ship their beef to market by rail. At the same time, the arrival of the railroad in the West was as much a boon to cattlemen as to the railroad companies. Yet for the cattleman's traditional way of life, it was the beginning of the end.

Before the Civil War, there had been no railways in cattle country, so cattlemen had to drive their herds either to the nearest shipping point—New Orleans—to be shipped expensively by boat, or drive them directly to whatever markets they could dig up in the West. When the railroads arrived after the war, cattlemen in Texas and other remote areas could drive their stock to a railhead for shipping to far more lucrative markets in the East.

The railroad shipping stations gave cattlemen an entirely new way to do business. Thus began the era of the great western cattle drive. Cattle trails soon ran from Texas northward into states and territories across the Great Plains. As cowboys drove thousands of herds freely across the open prairie, a legendary way of life emerged. In these early days, the Law of the Open Range was in full force. But by the mid-1870s, things were starting to change. The open range was being cut through by homesteaders and their barbed wire fences. And the railroads—at first such a godsend—were now contributing their own fences and accelerating the decline of the open range at breakneck speed. All along the old cattle routes, towns began to disappear.

The era of the great trail drives lasted only about fifteen years. During that time, cattlemen's relationship with the railroads changed drastically. As tracks went in throughout the West, the need to move cattle great distances disappeared. So ultimately, though the railroad was the reason that the cattle drives started, it was also the reason, in large part, that they ended.

The End of the Frontier

The railroad, in accordance with the federal government's policy to settle the West, was a key factor in turning the frontier into a profusion of towns, farms, and homesteads. By providing an economical way to transport people, animals, goods, and supplies between the East and the West, the railroad opened new markets for western meats, produce, and other products while also helping the growth of eastern suppliers.

The railroad companies owed much of their success to barbed wire. The innovation gave them a cheap and effective way to protect both settlers' livestock and their own passengers. Ultimately, barbed wire proved to be an indispensable tool for the railroad to assert its dominance over the American West.

Chicago & North Western Railway train carrying passengers and cargo into the west through several feet of snow. —FRED HULTSTRAND HISTORY AND PICTURES COLLECTION, NDIRS-NDSU, FARGO

Chapter 11

The Big Die-Up

y the early 1880s, the eastern portions of the American West—Kansas, Missouri, Nebraska, Arkansas, eastern Texas—had grown increasingly crowded. Cattlemen who had long been established in those parts grew weary of the changes and instability the newcomers brought with their eastern mindset and mazes of barbed wire. Many uprooted their operations and moved west to western Texas, Colorado, and Wyoming and Montana Territories, hoping to find a place where the Law of the Open Range still ruled.

The exodus of cattle operations from the more densely settled areas brought millions of head of livestock to the open country farther west. But many of these cattlemen were unfamiliar with the land and climate, and their livestock lacked the stamina to survive the extreme weather of the new ranges. In the punishing winter of 1885–86, these inexperienced cattlemen would face one of the costliest blows in the history of the American cattle industry.

Drifting Cattle

In a snowstorm, cattle would instinctively turn away from the torrent, always drifting south until they found a canyon or ravine to shelter them from the elements. Cowboys known as line riders kept the cattle from going too far astray, especially during the winter. Even during bitter cold spells, line riders worked the range, riding along the southern edge where the cattle were grazing and watering. The riders could not keep the cattle from drifting south; they simply followed the herd and did their best to keep its southern edge intact. In the spring, the line riders corralled the herd and directed it back north to the roundup, where owners could reclaim their stock.

As important as it was to keep track of drifting cattle, hiring line riders was expensive. Cattlemen began to seek a cheaper way to get the job done. In the early 1880s, some innovative cattlemen in the Texas Panhandle and elsewhere found what they thought was a solution. Perhaps ironically, it involved the use of the western cattleman's arch nemesis—barbed wire. To keep their cattle from straying too far south in the winter, they constructed drift fences—unconnected lines of barbed wire fencing—running east and west. These barriers essentially supplanted the job of the line riders at a cost of only $250 per mile.

Throughout 1881 and 1882, cattlemen of the Texas Panhandle erected drift fences on the open range. The two most prominent fences ran across the northern and southern edges of the Panhandle. The sections were long enough to block cattle but short enough not to close off the open range. The fences, cattlemen hoped, would not only keep their own cattle from drifting too far south but also prevent cattle farther north from encroaching on their range.

Barbed wire dealers and fellow cattlemen alike eagerly awaited the outcome of the Panhandle's large-scale experiment. By the end of the winter, it was apparent that the drift fences had accomplished precisely what the cattlemen hoped for. The results were so good that cattle owners built more drift fences the following year, and the fence building continued at a feverish pace for several more years. By the end of 1885 drift fences, laid out in ten- to forty-mile stretches, were staggered across the entire Texas Panhandle, from the edge of New Mexico Territory to the boundary of Indian Territory. With the completion of each section of drift fence, the jobs of more line riders disappeared.

Mother Nature Strikes

Just when cattlemen were applauding drift fences as a resounding success, matters took an ominous turn. In the winter of 1885–86, a series of unusually harsh blizzards struck the Great Plains, including the Texas Panhandle, where most of the drift fences stood. The first storm hit on New Year's Eve of 1885. It descended on the Great Plains with a howling gale that kept people indoors for several days. Then a second blizzard, worse than the first, struck a few days later. Before cattlemen could gather their forces to check the damage, a third snowstorm tore through the plains.

For several long frigid weeks, cattle owners could do little but sit and wonder how their cattle, left to fend for themselves, would withstand the severe weather. Livestock newly transplanted to the Panhandle from milder climates were especially at risk. One thing the cattlemen did not wonder was which direction their cattle would turn to escape the fury: south.

When the blizzards finally subsided, cattlemen and cowboys went out in search of their herds. What they found was devastation. All along the drift fences were dead cattle. For miles in both directions, some animals stood frozen in huddled groups, while others lay on their bellies and sides, piled up against the fences. Thousands of cattle had perished. According to some estimates, the losses ran as high as 200,000 head.

The cattle, instinctively heading away from the blizzards, could go no farther once they reached the drift fences. Some were lucky enough to skirt the barrier, but most stalled at the fence, milling back and forth against it. Without food, water, or shelter, the animals had little chance against the elements. Some froze in their tracks. Others stumbled over one another, piling into a great heap, suffocating those beneath. The devastation, which came to be known as the Big Die-Up, was most severe in the Panhandle, but all across the Great Plains the winter had been brutal, one of the worst on record.

When spring arrived, cattlemen in and around the Panhandle found their pastures bare of grass. During the winter, sheets of ice had covered large grazing areas, damaging the roots and slowing new growth. The little grass the cattle could paw through the snow to get at had been stripped bare.

In an effort to find grazing for their remaining cattle, Panhandle cattlemen trailed their herds as far north as Wyoming and Montana Territories. As a result, these northern regions became overstocked. To make matters worse, the spring weather, especially in Montana Territory, was unusually dry. As spring turned into summer, the severe drought continued, and what little grass that had come up now wilted. Temperatures in Montana and Wyoming Territories climbed to over a hundred degrees. Creeks and streams dried up, and rivers slowed to a trickle. The already weakened cattle grew more frail. With little fat or energy reserves, they were about to face another merciless winter.

Drift fences were still standing the following winter when another severe winter hit the West. In Montana Territory, temperatures dropped as low as thirty degrees below zero, and they stayed below zero through January and February 1887. Blizzards overtook the entire Great Plains, from Montana and Dakota Territories down to Indian Territory and Texas. Snowdrifts reached up to a hundred feet in places. President Theodore Roosevelt, who owned a ranch in Dakota Territory, noted that the barren land looked as though "it had been shaved with a razor."

Confined indoors again, people had little opportunity to feed and shelter their livestock, let alone rescue them from icy waters, canyons, and ravines. Many more cattle all across the West died of exposure or thirst. Desperate cattle ventured out onto sheets of ice to reach watering holes, only to tumble into the frigid water and drown. Others succumbed to attacks by coyotes and wolves.

Many cattle cut up their limbs on ice shards, and some lost their hooves to frostbite. Yet these losses numbered far fewer than those caused by drift fences.

In regions where drift fences still stood—including the Texas Panhandle and Wyoming Territory—livestock losses were even more devastating. Another Big Die-Up had struck. Many cattlemen estimated losses as high as 75 percent of their herds. In Wyoming Territory alone, more than $20 million worth of cattle perished that winter.

Tearing Down the Fences

In 1887, after two horrendous winters of severe livestock losses, cattlemen began the task of tearing down their barbed wire drift fences. Reeling from the catastrophe, they grew embittered and began a backlash against barbed wire. Protests that had first arisen more than a decade before, when barbed wire had made its debut, flared up anew. Those arguing against the inhumane effects of "the devil's rope" again raised their voices. Not surprisingly, line riders joined in the opposition, seizing the opportunity to try to regain their livelihoods. The strength of the agitation sent legislatures scrambling. Several states enacted laws to ban barbed wire or to restrict its use. The federal government assigned troops to the western territories to assist in removing unlawful fences.

Barbed wire manufacturers hurried to adjust their product. They needed new designs that would be effective yet less damaging to livestock. A rush of new applications flooded the U.S. Patent Office. The improved wires were designed so that cattle could easily recognize them and back away before making contact. Furthermore, if contact was made, the barbs were smaller and less vicious, designed to prick but not penetrate hides.

Over time, the improved barbed wire designs gained acceptance and eased tensions, and sales gradually rose again. Now it seemed that nothing could keep barbed wire from advancing across the West.

Chapter 12
Cattlemen Settle Down

By the late 1880s, it was obvious that the few cattlemen and cowboys who believed the West could return to the way it was before the arrival of barbed wire were sorely mistaken. By then, train tracks traversed the plains, towns were popping up everywhere, and, with the help of government, the fence builders had pretty much won the battle between Herd Law and the Law of the Open Range. For many, one of the most profound changes was the fading of cowboy traditions. Open range cattlemen were turning into landowning ranchers, and trail driving was well on its way to becoming an obsolete part of the cattle business.

The Decline of the Cattle Trail

From 1866 to 1880, hundreds of thousands of animals trod over western cattle trails on their way to market. In the summer of 1871, 700,000 Texas longhorns were driven to Kansas alone. But only a decade later, the number was down to 267,000. All along the way, cowboys on trail drives encountered barbed wire fences, often forcing them to find alternative routes. These obstacles increased with each passing year.

By the time the Texas legislature ruled fence cutting a felony in 1884, trail driving was already losing ground. By then, barbed wire drift fences were already going up in the Texas Panhandle, and the cattle route through Colorado had been truncated by homesteaders and their fences. Meanwhile, the expansion of the railroad meant more stations peppering the plains, so distances between cattle-raising areas and livestock shipping points grew ever shorter, rendering long trail drives unnecessary.

Other factors further damaged the practice of trail driving. Texas cow fever, a tick-borne disease that longhorn cattle were immune to, but that infected other cattle breeds, led to laws forbidding the passage of Texas cattle through Kansas and Missouri. To reinforce the prohibition, vigilantes in Kansas strung barbed wire and stood guard with six-guns to fend off Texas cattle drivers.

Despite the signs pointing to the death of trail driving, many in the cattle industry clung to the tradition. At the 1884 National Convention of Cattlemen in St. Louis, a proposal called for western cattlemen to pool their resources to buy a large tract of land as a national cattle trail, which would extend from Texas to the

Cowboys at mealtime during a trail drive of 3,500 head of cattle to the Oklahoma Panhandle, circa 1877. —COURTESY OF AMARILLO PUBLIC LIBRARY, PHOTOGRAPH BY TURTLES STUDIO

Canadian border. The cattlemen hoped to convince the federal government to contribute aid, reasoning that such a trail would lower the cost of meat for consumers. Although the proposal received considerable backing, and a bill was introduced in the House of Representatives in 1886, the effort ultimately failed.

Another proposal at the same time suggested a national lease law that would set aside federal lands for trail driving. The idea met with much resistance, however. Governor Ireland of Texas called the proposal an injustice to western settlers, saying it would compromise their rights to their homesteads. Others agreed, and like the national cattle trail bill, the lease law proposal failed.

By the mid-1880s, it had become clear to just about everyone that trail driving was coming to an end. Many once-thriving towns along the old cattle trails, such as Dodge City, Kansas, were already deserted. By the end of the decade, the American West was peopled and fenced from one end to the other. The notion of an unhindered range was gone, except in the memories of those who had seen it. The well-worn cattle trails and the life of the cowboy on the open range had all but disappeared.

Overcrowding on the Range

As time went on and settlers continued to claim public lands for homesteads, cattle operations were being forced to survive on smaller pastures. Cattlemen and their cowboys found themselves being squeezed out of the shrinking range. Eventually, many cattle owners in places like the Texas Panhandle and Kansas moved their operations into less densely settled parts of the West, such as Montana, Wyoming, and Dakota Territories, but even these regions were becoming too crowded for their comfort. By 1885 in Wyoming, barbed wire fences had already overrun the eastern part of the territory, compelling cattlemen to move their livestock west. At the same time in Montana Territory, settlers' barbed wire fences forced many cattlemen to graze their livestock at higher altitudes, where pastures were less than ideal.

As cattlemen flocked to these regions, pastures became overgrazed. Many local stockmen's associations took measures to counter the overcrowding. For example, in 1883 an association operating in Montana's Musselshell Valley published a notice in the *Helena Daily Herald* warning newcomers not to bring their herds there. Although the association could not legally prohibit new herds from grazing on public land, it could forbid arriving cattlemen to use its corrals or participate in its roundups, effectively keeping latecomers out of the area.

Cattlemen Use Barbed Wire

It became increasingly common for cattlemen in the West to put up barbed wire fences of their own. By the late 1880s, although some cattle owners still attempted to preserve the Law of the Open Range with stopgap measures to curb overcrowding, most started to accept that the fencing of the entire West was inevitable, and they knew that they would either have to join in on the land-grab or be left out in the cold.

The few cattlemen who could afford it purchased land and blocked it off with barbed wire fences. Many chose to lease

Cowboys stringing up barbed wire on posts (Minnesota, circa 1936). By the 1890s, cowboys were commonly seen working on ranches rather than out on the open range. —NATIONAL ARCHIVES AND RECORDS ADMINISTRATION

property for their cattle instead; they, too, fenced the boundaries with barbed wire. Either way, most cattlemen cut back on their operations, hiring fewer cowboys. The changes taking place in the West had already largely eliminated the tasks that had for so long occupied cowboys—line riding, trail driving, horse wrangling, and cattle herding. The role of the cowboy had gone from riding the open range to digging post holes and mending fences.

The Frying Pan and XIT Ranches

Astute barbed wire dealers observed the decline of the cattle drive and saw the handwriting on the wall. They knew it was only a matter of time before cattlemen realized that they had to join the barbed wire revolution if they were to remain in business. In 1881, the same year the fence cutting wars broke out, Joseph F. Glidden, the DeKalb man who had started it all by coming up with "the Winner," reemerged in the barbed wire business. Together with former Barb Fence Company salesman Henry Sanborn, Glidden purchased a large tract of land in the Texas Panhandle, where the partners would demonstrate the practicality of barbed wire to cattlemen. They aimed to create a fenced-in ranch.

The Frying Pan Ranch headquarters, built in 1881, was a six-room adobe house.
—COURTESY OF AMARILLO PUBLIC LIBRARY

They bought 250,000 acres, knowing that such a huge parcel would draw the attention of cattlemen everywhere. Using approximately 150 miles of Glidden's barbed wire, they fenced the entire area, at a cost of $39,000. Once the fence was completed, they enclosed within it 15,000 head of cattle. They called their ranch the Panhandle, but because the brand looked like a frying pan, the place became known as the Frying Pan Ranch.

The Frying Pan Ranch became a legendary success, proving without a doubt barbed wire's effectiveness in controlling pasture use, preserving herds, and reducing labor costs for cattlemen. In 1894 Glidden and Sanborn amicably dissolved their partnership. In the meantime, Sanborn developed an adjacent property into a town called Amarillo. Before long, Amarillo became one of the largest cattle-shipping stations in the world.

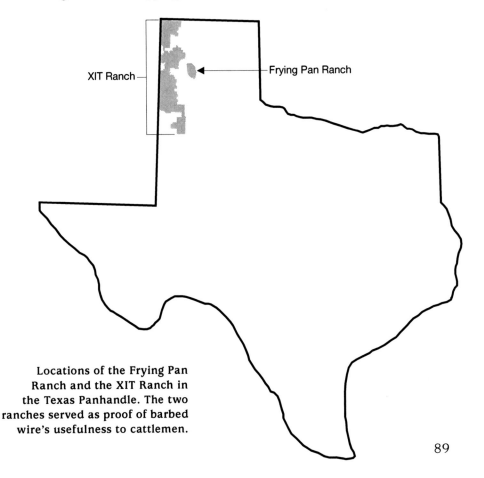

Locations of the Frying Pan Ranch and the XIT Ranch in the Texas Panhandle. The two ranches served as proof of barbed wire's usefulness to cattlemen.

89

Another ranching project—one that would also serve as a successful model of fencing for cattlemen—was in the works even as Glidden and Sanborn commenced the Frying Pan Ranch project. The XIT Ranch was constructed and fenced on over three million acres of the Texas Panhandle. The ranch covered twenty-seven miles from east to west, and stretched two hundred miles north to south. Construction of the ranch began in 1883, and by July 1885 ranch workers had fenced 476,000 acres, the largest area in the country under barbed wire. It had taken 300 workers and $7 million to erect 3,000 miles of barbed wire fencing. By late 1886, the ranch had 110,721 head of longhorn cattle, which cost $1,332,587. The XIT gained the reputation not only of the largest ranch in the American West, but also of the world's largest fenced-in range in the nineteenth century.

The End of the Open Range

The successful application of barbed wire fences at the Frying Pan Ranch, the XIT Ranch, and other cattle outfits in the Texas Panhandle overcame all doubts that barbed wire was an effective tool for cattlemen, just as it was for farmers and railroad companies. Many cattlemen who once rode the open range, slept under the stars, and kept watch over free-roaming cattle turned themselves into ranchers. They began buying up land in earnest and fencing in their pastures. It was a turning point in the cattle industry.

Realizing that the days of the open range were coming to an end, these cattlemen who fenced in their operations hastened the inevitable by jumping on the barbed wire bandwagon. Rather than find themselves evicted from their own beloved West, they chose to swim with the tide. The notion of private land ownership in the American West soon became as accepted among cattlemen as the changing of the seasons.

A herd of cattle within a fenced corral, probably in Colorado, sometime between 1886 and 1901. —DENVER PUBLIC LIBRARY, ROSE AND HOPKINS, WESTERN HISTORY COLLECTION, H-608

Chapter 13
Native Lands Corralled

As barbed wire created dramatic physical changes across the western landscape, cattlemen and cowboys were not the only population that had to adapt. By the late 1880s, Native Americans were feeling barbed wire's impact even in the far reaches of the West. The consequences of barbed wire, combined with the federal government's policy of opening up their native lands to white settlement, made it impossible for Indians in the West to preserve their traditional way of life.

From Native Lands to Reservations

Many tribes living in the West after 1840 had been forcibly relocated there from the East by federal troops to make way for white settlement. In 1825 President James Monroe spoke of moving all Indians out of the eastern United States to "vacant" lands west of the Mississippi. By the time barbed wire arrived in the mid-1870s, this had been accomplished.

The Five Civilized Tribes, as they were referred to by whites—the Creek, Chickasaw, Cherokee, Seminole, and Choctaw tribes—were among those forced into Indian Territory, roughly present-day Oklahoma, in the 1830s. The government also relocated other tribes to Indian Territory during this period. But in the West, until the mid-1800s, some tribes still roamed their native ranges, hunting the buffalo that traveled along their natural migratory routes. Other western tribes also followed seasonal routes to gather plants; still others traveled regularly to trade with other tribes.

But for the Plains Indians, life as they knew it was changing. Even before the introduction of barbed wire, tribes were being pushed off their homelands to make room for white settlement. The 1851 Indian Appropriations Act instituted a reservation system for many western tribes. For the affected tribes, the relocation, often accomplished by force, destroyed their nomadic traditions.

Barbed Wire Blocks Indian Routes

The success of barbed wire fences in the 1870s and beyond meant that Native Americans increasingly encountered signs of white settlement on lands that had once been open. For tribes who had not already been placed on reservations by the mid-1870s, barbed wire finished the job the federal government had started.

Comanche buffalo hunters in front of their teepees (circa 1871).
—COURTESY OF THE NATIONAL ARCHIVES AND RECORDS ADMINISTRATION

Some Plains tribes had resisted the government's efforts to relocate them, and the mid-1800s saw numerous violent confrontations west of the Mississippi. When barbed wire fences appeared on the range, eventually enveloping the West with a dizzying network of barriers, the natives found themselves increasingly corralled. Routes Native Americans had traveled for centuries became inaccessible.

Col. Charles Goodnight, who established the first major cattle trail in 1866, told of an encounter he had with a group of New Mexican Pueblo Indians in the Texas Panhandle in 1878 and 1879—only a few years after Glidden invented "the Winner." After diffusing a tense situation the Pueblos had been facing with a group of settlers, Goodnight stayed to converse with them. He was shocked when the Pueblo chief asked Goodnight if he would direct them back to Taos. How could they be lost in an area they'd traveled for years? Goodnight finally uncovered the root of the Pueblos' confusion: barbed wire fences all along the Pueblo trade route blocked their normal passage.

Blocking the Buffalo

Besides disrupting native trade and food-gathering routes, barbed wire fences hastened the near extinction of the American buffalo by blocking the herds' migratory routes. The buffalo herds of the Great Plains had already been severely depleted by white hunters and settlers, who often killed them indiscriminately. The U.S. Army was known to have used buffalo as practice targets for soldiers on horseback. Some people have suggested that it was the federal government's policy to kill off buffalo as a way to devastate Indians in the West.

Buffalo populations dropped significantly in the 1870s and 1880s. In 1800, sixty-five million buffalo roamed the West, but by 1865—three years after the enactment of the Homestead Act—those numbers had fallen to fifteen million. By 1890, when barbed wire fence building was in full swing, fewer than a thousand buffalo remained in the American West. Throughout this steady decline, natives had to travel over ever-widening areas to seek out the buffalo that had once been so plentiful. Barbed wire only made hunting more difficult.

Barbed Wire and the Cherokee Outlet

By the 1880s, some Native Americans were beginning to accept barbed wire fences, and even to erect fences themselves. Some Indians took to raising cattle or farming and used barbed wire fences the same way settlers did. In Indian Territory, some tribes helped construct fencing for oil companies carrying out mineral and oil exploration on reservation land. And along the northern boundary of Indian Territory, in a section of land known as the Cherokee Outlet, the Cherokees allowed cattlemen to erect barbed wire fences on land the cattlemen leased from the tribe.

Beginning in the 1860s, cattlemen trailed thousands of cattle through Indian Territory on their way from Texas to Kansas and Missouri. In 1866 cattlemen drove approximately six hundred thousand head through the Cherokee Outlet. The Cherokees, seeing an opportunity for profit, began levying taxes on cattle driven through their lands. The taxes were deemed lawful, and by 1882 the tribe had collected tens of thousands of dollars.

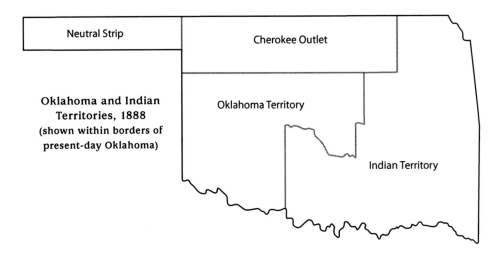

Neutral Strip

Cherokee Outlet

Oklahoma and Indian Territories, 1888 (shown within borders of present-day Oklahoma)

Oklahoma Territory

Indian Territory

Furthermore, the Cherokees noticed that some cattlemen lingered on the Outlet to take advantage of the grazing pastures there, so the tribe began imposing a permit system for grazing. Some cattlemen even paid to maintain permanent herds in the territory. For the most part, cattlemen willingly complied with the new rules. A group called the Cherokee Strip Livestock Association, composed mostly of Kansas cattlemen, was especially supportive of the arrangement.

Some cattlemen who maintained permanent herds on the Cherokee Outlet erected barbed wire fences to guard their livestock. The Indians did not object to this, since it allowed them to monitor the herds in the territory and better determine the fees due to them. The Cherokees also often put into the lease agreement that when the cattlemen left, the fences became the property of the tribe.

Soon, however, many cattlemen driving their herds through the Cherokee Outlet became frustrated by the other cattlemen's fences, which blocked passage along cattle trails. Complaints against barbed wire fencing in Indian Territory, particularly against the Cherokee Strip Livestock Association, grew increasingly vocal. In 1882 the federal government investigated the complaints. In a reversal of its previous position, the government declared that it did not recognize the permits and called the barbed wire fencing in the Cherokee Outlet unauthorized. It directed that livestock owners in the Cherokee Outlet remove all cattle and all improvements—including barbed wire fences—within twenty days or the government would dispatch troops to tear them down.

Many of the cattlemen with fences in the Outlet objected to the government's demand, protesting that twenty days was an insufficient time in which to comply. Others simply defied the order—in 1883 the Cherokees and the Cherokee Strip Livestock Association agreed to a five-year lease for $100,000 per year. The association divided the leased land into more than a hundred tracts to be subleased to individual cattlemen and organizations.

In an 1883 report, the federal government noted that nearly a thousand miles of barbed wire fencing was still present in the Outlet. Eventually, in response to the overwhelming protests of the rent-paying cattlemen, the government revised its original order. It would allow barbed wire fences already built in the Outlet to remain standing, but no new fences could be erected.

Meanwhile, however, settlers had been pressuring the federal government to open up Indian Territory to homestead claims. Some settlers—called boomers—already illegally occupied land in the Cherokee Outlet. Though the government periodically ordered them out, the presence of boomers added to the tensions over fencing the land. The dispute between cattlemen and settlers was not so much about whether or not Indian Territory should be fenced, but about who should be allowed to fence it.

The conflict over the use of land in the Cherokee Outlet continued until the government issued a final order in 1890. The Secretary of the Interior took the position that the Cherokees had never really owned the Outlet in the first place, but in fact had owned only an easement. He then concluded that the tribe had lost their right to the easement because the Indians did not personally use it. Therefore, the Cherokees lacked the authority to levy taxes or issue grazing permits. The Attorney General agreed with the secretary's conclusion, and President Benjamin Harrison ordered that all improvements—barbed wire fences and houses put up by cattlemen—be torn down. To ensure that his orders were carried out, he sent federal troops to the region.

As a result of that decision, the government essentially disallowed any productive use of the Cherokee Outlet by the tribe. In December 1891 the Cherokee Nation relinquished its rights to the Outlet for $8.5 million. Two years later, the government opened some of the Cherokee Outlet to white settlement, creating the biggest land rush in the nation's history.

The settlers had won out. Cattlemen were no longer allowed to graze livestock in Indian Territory, and Native Americans no longer had use of the Cherokee Outlet, which became part of Oklahoma Territory.

The Dawes General Allotment Act

In 1887 Congress furthered its goal of turning the West into agricultural land with the passage of the Dawes General Allotment Act. The Dawes Act attempted to assimilate natives into white culture by breaking up reservations into 160-acre parcels and allotting the parcels to individual Indians rather than to tribes. The Dawes Act had the effect of breaking up the social structure of the tribes, who lived communally.

For the most part, the law's objective to turn Native Americans into farmers was a failure. Many tribes resisted the agricultural way of life, even though their traditional method of subsistence—primarily buffalo hunting—was increasingly unavailable. Moreover, the 160-acre parcels were inadequate for farming, for much of the land parceled out to individual Indians had very poor soil.

The federal government, however, was concerned less about the failure of Indian farming and more about the freeing up of reservation land for white settlement. After parceling out individual lots to Indians, the government conveniently found that there was "surplus" land. The Dawes Act had provided that surplus reservation land would be available to white settlers, who took full advantage of it.

From 1893 onward, the government opened up section after section of Indian Territory to white settlement, and with each instance tribes found themselves confined to increasingly smaller areas. Like the cattlemen and cowboys, Native Americans lost their ability to travel across a range that had once stretched out wide and open. Their lands had been seized by white settlers and fenced with barbed wire.

Chapter 14

Fencing Free-for-All

By the end of the 1880s, fencing was an expected sight across the western landscape. Cattlemen were quickly coming to accept that fences were replacing the open range, and they looked for ways to secure their livelihoods under these new conditions. Of prime importance were adequate grazing and watering areas.

Big cattlemen could well afford to purchase land in large tracts to provide grazing and water for their herds, and they did so in increasing numbers. But most small cattlemen were less fortunate. They did not have the means to purchase enough land to sustain their herds. Even if they could afford land, it was hard to find property with adequate access to water. In some cases, cattlemen who owned land with a stream or river would use so much water that the land downstream became too dry for cattle.

These conditions in the cattle industry created a climate ripe for lawlessness. With their livelihoods at stake, many less affluent cattlemen resorted to illegally claiming and fencing land they did not own. Even the bigger cattlemen often chose the less costly way out and did the same thing.

False Claims and Land Seizures

One of the most common ways cattlemen illegally acquired land was through false claims. Some cattlemen simply filed claims under the Homestead Act using assumed names. Others would legally claim one plot, then send their employees to file homestead claims for adjacent plots. Later, the employees "sold" the land back to the cattleman.

The way cattlemen saw matters, the false claims were justified because the public lands that had once been part of the vast, open range had been unfairly taken from them. They had already tried to accomplish their ends through legitimate channels—offering proposals and petitioning for favorable legislature—but these efforts had failed.

In many cases, cattlemen simply put up barbed wire fences around public land they wanted for themselves. This illegal seizing of public lands was a rampant problem wherever such lands still existed. This type of land-grabbing festered in pockets throughout the West beginning in the early 1880s, and the problem mounted into the 1890s.

The worst period of illegal land-grabbing occurred in 1887 and 1888, with fence building violations becoming as widespread as fence cutting had been in the early 1880s. In Colorado, for example, estimates show that one million acres were under illegal fence enclosure in the late 1880s, and most of that land was public property. In 1887, at the peak of illegal fencing, approximately ten million acres of land had been illegally fenced. Illegal fence building was so severe during this period that it even impeded the delivery of mail. In discussing the problem, the commissioner of the General Land Office of the Department of the Interior said that it was "doubtful if the world has ever witnessed such criminal prodigality."

Homesteading farmers and newly arriving settlers in the West protested the illegal land-grabbing. Much of the public land that settlers hoped to claim under the Homestead Act was, in practical terms, unavailable to them. But government authorities—whether local, state, or federal—responded sluggishly to settlers' requests for intervention.

Farmers Join the Land-Grab

Cattlemen were not the only ones guilty of illegal land-grabbing. Settlers also had a motivation to seize land unlawfully. The practice had been going on since the 1862 Homestead Act, which granted 160 acres to any citizen willing to settle on the plot for five years and make improvements on it. Many settlers discovered that 160 acres was inadequate for a viable farm. In the West, it took anywhere from twenty-five to one hundred acres to produce the same quantity of crops that farmers could cultivate on ten to fifteen acres in the East's grassy meadows.

By the 1880s, two laws existed that were meant to boost settlers' ability to make an adequate living from their land claims. The Desert Land Act of 1877 allowed for 320-acre claims on arid land. Still, this acreage was often inadequate. With the cost and time required to irrigate the homestead, it was seldom worthwhile to pursue the claim. The second law was the Timber and Stone Act of 1878, which allowed for 320-acre land grants in areas where timber, stone, or both made agricultural cultivation challenging. Again, however, 320 acres was usually insufficient.

While some settlers tried to make do with what the standing laws offered, others sought to increase their land holdings using whatever means—legal or not—that they could. And like some land-grabbing cattlemen, some settlers claimed more land simply because they could get away with it. As more farmers and cattlemen joined in, the land-grabbing became a self-perpetuating force.

Political Maneuvering

During the fence cutting wars of the early 1880s, much of the population of the West was composed of cattlemen, who held most of the political power. Public sentiment at the time had sided heavily with these protectors of the open range, even if the government did not. But by the late 1880s, the number of homesteaders had increased enough that public opinion turned in favor of the settlers. The issue of fencing versus not fencing had become moot, and everyone was fencing the land. Now the question was, who had the right to fence it? As lawless land-grabbing reached a frenzy, the settlers turned their attention to stopping cattlemen from taking land that they believed was rightfully theirs to claim.

Propaganda during this period painted a negative picture of cattlemen. The Farmers' Alliance, a political organization that worked for economic conditions and policies favorable to farmers, pushed the notion that the remaining public lands belonged to the people and should be dedicated as homesteads to settlers. The phrase "the children's grass," referring to the Great Plains, emerged around that time to suggest that greedy cattle barons were taking for themselves the rightful heritage of future generations.

Settlers attempted to maneuver their way through the political world. Many submitted complaints and petitions to local, state, and federal authorities across the West, and throughout the mid-1880s and beyond they continued to file pleas for government intervention. Some hired lawyers with the hope that their legal expertise would aid their cause.

Cattlemen were not without their own political tactics. Many large cattlemen, individually and through powerful livestock associations, were already influential with governors and legislators. Cattlemen also employed lobbyists who fought to protect cattlemen's rights and defeat any attempt to break up their interests.

While cattlemen and farmers battled each other through political channels, barbed wire manufacturers also entered the fray. Manufacturers gave freely to campaign chests in state and national elections. They hoped to dissuade any legislative action that might negatively impact the demand for their product. In some instances, manufacturers succeeded in getting their own industry executives elected to high office.

Factories such as this one owned by Jacob Haish in DeKalb, Illinois, operated feverishly to meet the increasing demand for legal and illegal barbed wire across the American West. —COURTESY OF THE JOINER HISTORY ROOM, SYCAMORE, ILLINOIS

Violence Erupts

As cattlemen and settlers illegally fenced off lands, violence and crime reminiscent of the fence cutting wars resurfaced. Just as the fence cutting wars had erupted in Texas in 1881 and then spread, clashes between perpetrators and opponents of illegal fence building broke out in stages, not all at once. The occurrence of violence depended on the degree of settlement. This cycle—increased settlement, followed by mounting friction, then violence—spread throughout the West.

During the late 1880s, trouble typically began with the destruction of illegal fences. Unlike the fence cutting wars earlier in the decade, in which cattlemen and their cowboys were cutting down settlers' fences, in the illegal fence conflicts settlers were most often the main culprits, destroying cattlemen's fences and cutting down barbed wire wherever it appeared on public lands.

Some farmers did more than cut down fences. They shot at cattle that roamed onto their crop fields, and some even shot at cattlemen and cowboys suspected of illegal fence building. Many big cattlemen, in turn, did not hesitate to assert their power. They shot at farmers who threatened or harmed their livestock. In retaliation against settlers they suspected of cutting down their fences, some big cattlemen sent out their employees to farmers' homesteads to destroy the farmers' property. They also struck at farmers' livelihoods by burning their crop fields. While they fought back against settlers, cattlemen continued building fences around lands they had seized.

The illegal fence conflict highlighted an attitude shift among cattlemen. While cattlemen big and small had united against settlers' barbed wire fences from the mid-1870s through the early 1880s, by the late 1880s, barbed wire became a source of division between the owners of big cattle operations and those of smaller ones.

Many cattlemen built fences not only to keep settlers away, but also to block off fellow cattlemen. Small operators—owners of only a few hundred head of cattle—generally could not afford to buy enough land to keep up their herds, while bigger cattlemen bought up—or illegally seized—all the land they could, effectively squeezing the small guys out. Many small cattlemen felt that their only option was violence. They burned big cattlemen's fences and property, rustled their herds, stole their horses, and shot their livestock. In some cases, they even went so far as to kill people.

As the conflict heated up, farmers in some areas banded together with small cattlemen to fight the power of big cattlemen, organizing into groups that systematically tore down the fences of big cattle operations. In Custer County, Nebraska, for example, settlers were so enraged by one rancher's illegal fencing that five hundred of them organized and, in one night in 1885, destroyed fifteen miles of barbed wire fence around the Brighton Ranch.

Rustlers took advantage of the chaos of the illegal fence frenzy, just as they had during the fence cutting wars. Most rustlers were indiscriminate, stealing from settlers and cattlemen alike, using their booty to create their own herds. Some rustlers, however, chose to ally with homesteaders in destroying the fences of big cattlemen, using these opportunities to rustle livestock.

The Government Chooses Sides

In the mid-1880s, settlers' complaints against illegal fencing by cattlemen began to get results. In 1885 President Grover Cleveland issued a proclamation ordering all unlawful enclosures removed from public lands. He directed the U.S. Marshal to send forces to take down illegal fences. His proclamation also forbade threats and intimidations against settlers on public land.

Despite the presidential mandate, it proved difficult—virtually impossible—for federal authorities to accomplish their task. In most cases, they had to first prove that a homestead claim was fraudulent before they could tear down any fences. Government inspectors were often fooled by makeshift improvements on a false homestead claim. A cattleman with multiple false claims might move a single hastily built dwelling to his various homestead sites for the purpose of inspection—some cabins were actually put on wheels.

President Benjamin Harrison, who succeeded Cleveland, adopted the same course of action as his predecessor. Cleveland was reelected in 1892 and picked up where he left off, pursuing settlers' rights in the West. In 1895 the General Land Office began resurveying land in the West—particularly in Nebraska, where much illegal fence building occurred. The resurveying allowed the government to determine the location of actual homestead claims and check their improvements, including fences.

Using information from the surveys and other evidence, the federal government prosecuted some illegal fence builders in the federal courts. Once this happened, far fewer outbreaks of fence cutting and property destruction occurred. But illegal fencing continued for years, even into the twentieth century. As late as 1901, President Theodore Roosevelt declared, "The fences must come down. It is illegal to enclose government land, you varmints."

In the end, though it took a long time to fully enforce, the federal government gave the right of occupancy to law-abiding settlers. It became clear at last to both illegal fence cutters and illegal fence builders that the government would not hesitate to exercise its powers in favor of settlers. From Indian relocation to taking down illegal fences, government intervention on behalf of the farming settlers was key to the transformation of the West from open range to fenced-in farms and ranches.

Chapter 15

The New Face of the West

The use of barbed wire by settlers and cattlemen gained momentum through the 1890s and into the new century. Demand for the product accelerated, and due to industrial advances it became increasingly affordable. When first introduced in 1874, barbed wire sold for as high as twenty cents per pound. By 1885 the price had fallen to eighteen cents per pound, and with each passing year prices continued to drop. By 1893 barbed wire cost as little as two cents per pound. Meanwhile, production increased dramatically. In 1875 annual production was 270 tons; by 1901 that amount had grown to 135,000 tons.

Barbed wire transformed not only the landscape of the American West but also the lives of its occupants in the last quarter of the nineteenth century. For Plains Indians, barbed wire marked an end to many tribes' nomadic way of life by accelerating the white man's grasp on the land. For cattlemen and cowboys, it replaced their traditional life on the open range with ranches. For settlers, it granted the power to control and protect the land they farmed, making homesteading a more feasible endeavor.

From Conflict to Confluence

Once the heat of the fence cutting wars and the illegal fence building frenzy had cooled, both cattlemen and settlers set to work on developing the best practices for thriving in the new western landscape. The needs of settlers and of landowning cattlemen were no longer in direct conflict and, in fact, shared much in common. Cattlemen settled down and became ranchers, and found it expedient to grow grain for their livestock. Settlers also raised livestock, sometimes expanding their land holdings to accommodate grazing cattle. The line between farmers and ranchers became less distinct.

When settlers first arrived in the West, they learned a great deal from the cattlemen about how to survive. Water in many parts of the West was a scarcity to be treasured, and anyone living there had to learn how to make use of what little water there was. Cattlemen had been drilling wells, pumping water with windmills, and irrigating the semiarid plains of the American West even when it was open range, long before the onslaught of settlers. Settlers adopted these same practices out of necessity. Settlers in some areas also recognized that it often served their purposes to raise some cattle. With ownership of livestock, settlers came to partially understand the traditional open range customs that were suited to the land. Thus the settlers in the West lived on the land very differently than farmers in the East, and much more like western ranchers.

Barbed wire contributed its part. It enabled settlers to divide the land into the most efficient manner to observe proper crop rotation. It also allowed them to separate livestock from crop fields during the growing season. In addition, barbed wire made it possible to use the same fields as grazing pasture after harvest.

Cattlemen Turned Ranchers

In the final decade of the 1800s, most cattlemen altered their practices to adapt to the crowding and fencing of the West. They bought land and built permanent ranch buildings, and the workers spent minimal time wandering the ranges with cattle herds. These new ranchers erected their own barbed wire enclosures to protect their property and to keep their cattle within their appointed grazing grounds. The Frying Pan and XIT Ranches of the 1880s were the first widely known examples of fully fenced ranches, and they provided successful models for cattlemen. In short, cattlemen became settlers, though on a scale large enough for cattle raising.

Even those cattlemen who had retreated into the most remote corners of the West eventually had to follow suit. By accepting and ultimately embracing barbed wire as an essential tool of their trade, cattlemen joined settlers—their former enemies—in bringing about the irreversible changes in the West.

Ranchers adopted other practices of settlers. In addition to grazing their livestock in enclosed fields, they grew crops as supplementary feed. This was necessary, as cattle could no longer roam far and wide to graze on prairie grasses. When winter arrived on the plains, ranchers had stored enough feed to keep

Workers in Osnabrock, North Dakota, using a chain-driven engine to separate grain from straw for cattle feed (circa 1890s). By the late 1890s, most cattlemen in the West had become ranchers, growing supplementary feed for their livestock. —COURTESY OF FRED HULTSTRAND HISTORY IN PICTURES COLLECTION, NDIRS-NDSU, FARGO

their livestock nourished, avoiding the risks of having cattle wander out on the range in harsh weather. Stock owners had far less worry about massive winter losses due to exposure or starvation, as in the big die-ups of the 1880s.

Increased Profits

In the end, western cattlemen discovered that barbed wire may have turned out to be their best friend. Raising cattle in a confined area had a number of significant benefits. Livestock that wandered less grew fatter. Growing feed also made cattle fatter and kept them healthier, resulting in an overall higher grade of product that commanded higher prices. In addition, confining cattle reduced loss due to straying, rustling, and other hazards of the open range, including starvation and thirst, extreme weather, and predators.

Fencing up livestock reduced costs not only by reducing losses, but also by largely eliminating the need for branding. On the open range, branding had been essential to identify which cattle belonged to whom. A unique, recognizable brand that was difficult to mask could thwart rustlers, but as the century neared its end, it was difficult to originate a new brand because so many already existed. More important, however, was the cost of branding. In 1886 the Tanners Association of America concluded that the collective time cattlemen devoted to branding cost $15 million per year. With barbed wire fences to enclose their livestock, ranchers saved much time and money by not having to brand.

Ranchers could also use barbed wire to control cattle breeding. They could keep cows and bulls separated and choose which ones to breed. Thus they could increase the likelihood of getting large and robust offspring, which would produce more meat and bring them more profit. Ranchers could also choose the time of year to breed. Timing the mating allowed ranchers to ensure that calves were born during warmer months, giving them a better chance of survival during the winter. Barbed wire enclosures could also be used to control the weaning of calves. Ranchers separated calves from their mothers in the autumn, which improved the survival rates of cows during the winter by eliminating the stress of nursing calves.

Industrial and Population Growth

As more and more Americans settled and began farming the West, and as the cattle-raising industry adapted its operations to privately owned lands, the country grew at a remarkable pace. Unlike in the 1860s and 1870s, when many of the new arrivals in the West were gold seekers, railroad workers, cowboys, soldiers, and other bachelors, many settlers in the 1880s and 1890s were families, coming west for permanent settlement. By 1900, seventeen million Americans resided in the West, compared with seven hundred thousand in 1840.

The population growth, expedited by the railroads, brought infrastructure and stability. Small communities, complete with

By the end of the nineteenth century, communities in the West had grown significantly, creating the need for schools such as this one in North Dakota (1896).
—FRED HULTSTRAND HISTORY IN PICTURES COLLECTION, NDIRS-NDSU, FARGO

schoolhouses, churches, restaurants, general stores, and other businesses, sprouted up all across the West. Slaughterhouses and meat-packing plants arose in the western states, eliminating the need to transport livestock great distances. The development of refrigerated railcars enabled slaughterhouses to load meat onto trains bound for eastern cities.

Towns continued to prosper under these new conditions, and as a result, land in the American West gained value. In Texas, for example, land increased in value by more than 100 percent between 1865 and 1900.

Between the end of the Civil War and the end of the nineteenth century, the American economy matured into an agricultural-industrial economy. The increase in farming operations in the American West coupled with the growing American population, which demanded more food products, further spurred eastern businesses to invent and manufacture machines that farmers could use to grow and harvest crops with more ease and in greater quantities. From 1870 to 1900, U.S. agricultural production doubled, and the expansion of farming and ranching in the West played a significant part in that growth.

Barbed wire turned a corner and there was no going back. The end of the open range and the establishment of agriculture changed the physical, economic, and social framework of the West. Gone were the cattle drives, gone was the wandering cowboy, gone was the open range. Here to stay were farmers, homesteads, and fields of corn and wheat. Here to stay were ranchers, the transformed cattlemen of the West, who raised cattle in barbed wire enclosures, grew feed for their livestock on their own pastures, and settled on their ranches. A simple twist of the wire had forever changed America.

Appendix A

Sites of Interest

Devil's Rope Museum. Bills itself as the largest barbed wire museum in the world. 100 Kingsley Street, P.O. Box 290, McLean, Texas 79057, (806) 779-2225, www.barbwire museum.com

Ellwood House and Museum. Isaac L. Ellwood's Victorian mansion, built in 1879. Museum offers tours. 509 North First Street, DeKalb, Illinois 60115, www.ellwoodhouse.org

Glidden Homestead and Historical Center. Joseph F. Glidden's house, built in the 1860s. Where Glidden designed his barbed wire, "the Winner." 921 W. Lincoln Hwy., DeKalb, Illinois 60115, (815) 756-7904, www.gliddenhomestead.org

Homestead National Monument of America. National park in Nebraska dedicated to the Homestead Act of 1862. National Park Service, U.S. Department of the Interior, www .nps.gov/home

Jacob Haish Mfg. Co. Web site dedicated to Jacob Haish's contributions. www.jacobhaishmfg.org

Kansas Barbed Wire Museum. Dedicated to the history of barbed wire in the American West. 120 W. 1st Street, LaCrosse, Kansas 67548, (785) 222-9900, www.rushcounty .org/BarbedWireMuseum/BWhistory.htm

Library of Congress. Online exhibit, "America's Story from America's Library: The Homestead Act Went into Effect May 20, 1862." www.americaslibrary.gov/cgi-bin/pagc.cgi/jb/civil/homested_1

National Archives. Online exhibit, "Teaching with Documents: The Homestead Act of 1862." The U.S. National Archives and Records Administration, www.archives.gov/education/lessons/homestead-act

Smithsonian Institution. National Museum of American History. Online exhibit, "Barbed Wire, the Thorny Fence that Transformed the West." Lemelson Center, Smithsonian Institution, www.inventionatplay.org/inventors_bar.html#

XIT Museum. Contains exhibits illustrating the history of the XIT Ranch and the American West. Also houses art gallery. 108 East 5th Street, Dalhart, Texas 79022, (806) 244-5390, www.xitmuseum.com

Appendix B

Resources for Collectors

Antique Barbed Wire Society. An international organization in La Crosse, Kansas, committed to collecting, preserving, and interpreting the historical heritage of barbed wire and related items. They have books, art prints, and wire available for purchase online. 2720 Camino Chueco, Santa Fe, New Mexico 87505-5250, treasabws@gmail.com, www.antique barbedwiresociety.com

The Barbed Wire Collector. A bimonthly magazine published by the Antique Barbed Wire Society. Each issue has a variety of information about all things related to barbed wire collecting, including books, auctions and shows, fencing tools, fence posts, salesman samples, and classified ads. www .antiquebarbedwiresociety.com/magazine.html

Colorado Wire Collector's Association. Contact Shawn Kirscht, 236 East 6th Street, Walsenburg, Colorado 81089, (719) 738-1365 or (719) 989-0201, barbedwire5@aol.com

Devil's Rope Museum. Billed as the largest barbed wire historic museum in the world. The Web site information for collectors includes history, wire identification, events and activities, and recommended books. 100 Kingsley Street, P.O. Box 290, McLean, Texas 79057, (806) 779-2225, www .barbwiremuseum.com

Kansas Barbed Wire Collectors Association. Operates the Kansas Barbed Wire Museum. P.O. Box 578, LaCrosse, Kansas 67548-0578. A membership application is available at www.rushcounty.org/BarbedWireMuseum/BWmember.htm

Kansas Barbed Wire Museum. This museum in La Crosse, Kansas, exhibits over 2,000 types of barbed wire, including some manufactured between 1870 and 1890, as well as hundreds of antique fencing tools. The museum houses the Larry Greer Research Center, which has the largest known collection of patents related to barbed wire and fencing tools. 120 W. 1st Street, LaCrosse, Kansas 67548, www.rushcounty.org/BarbedWireMuseum

Nebraska Barbed Wire Collectors Association. Contact John Stohlmann, 6006 North 168th Street, Omaha, Nebraska 68116-3806, (402) 964-9797, okkate@cox.net

New Mexico Barbed Wire Collectors Association. Contact Dan and Nancy Sowle, P.O. Box 102, Stanley, New Mexico 87056-0102, (505) 832-4339, nsowle@wildblue.net

Northern Rocky Mountain Barbed Wire Collectors, Inc. Contact Glade Wasden, P.O. Box 385, Rexburg, Idaho 83440, (208) 356-3362, marilyn@ida.net

Chronology

1840   Fewer than 700,000 citizens populate the American West.

1841   Congress passes the Preemption Act, allowing settlers to occupy government land without first paying for it, and giving them the right to buy the land later at a low cost.

1850   Passage of the Donation Land Law allows settlers to claim 640 acres of free land in Oregon Territory if the claimants cultivate the land for four consecutive years.

1851   The phrase "Go west, young man" becomes something of a national motto urging people to move west and settle the frontier.

1857   First known use of barbed wire in the country: John Grinninger of Texas tops his garden fence with string of homemade barbed wire.

1861   American Civil War begins.

1862   The Homestead Act is signed into law, offering 160 acres of public land free to settlers who build on and cultivate the claim for five years.

   The Pacific Railway Act is passed, enabling the construction of a transcontinental railroad.

1865   American Civil War ends. Homesteaders begin migration to the West in earnest.

1866   A. T. Kelly of Peoria, Illinois, patents the first all-metal barb in the United States.

Col. Charles Goodnight blazes the first major cattle trail, the Goodnight-Loving Trail, driving 2,000 longhorns from Texas to New Mexico.

1867   Barbed wire makes its official appearance on the continent in three variations: Alphonso Dabb's "picketed wrought iron strip," Lucien B. Smith's "wire fencing armed with projecting point," and William D. Hunt's spur-wheel design.

1869   Transcontinental railroad is completed.

1871   The U.S. government issues a report confirming the lack of effective, practical fencing as a serious problem in the West.

During the summer season, 700,000 Texas longhorns are driven to Kansas.

1873   Henry Rose displays his barbed fence attachment design at the DeKalb County fair.

Farmer Joseph Glidden creates his own design of barbed wire in DeKalb, Illinois, after viewing Henry Rose's exhibit at a county fair. Glidden applies for a patent in October. His will eventually become the most successful barbed wire design, earning it the nickname "the Winner."

Lumberman Jacob Haish, also inspired by Rose's fair exhibit, designs several variations of barbed wire and applies for a patent for his first barbed wire design in December.

1874   Haish receives a patent for his first barbed wire design in January, and he applies for a patent for his "S" barb design in June.

Haish files interference papers against Glidden, beginning the feud over who has the right to manufacture and sell barbed wire.

Glidden receives the patent for "the Winner" design in November.

Glidden sells 50 percent of his interest in "the Winner" to Isaac L. Ellwood, and they form the Barb Fence Company. The company sells 10,000 pounds of barbed wire in its first year.

1875   Henry B. Sanborn and J. P. Warner travel to Texas as barbed wire salesmen for the Barb Fence Company, but they are unsuccessful at opening up the Texas market.

The Barb Fence Company manufactures and sells more than 600,000 pounds of barbed wire.

Haish receives a patent for his "S" barb design.

1876   John "Bet-a-Million" Gates stages a successful demonstration at San Antonio Military Plaza to display barbed wire's effectiveness in deterring livestock.

Glidden sells his remaining 50 percent interest to Washburn & Moen Company. The Barb Fence Company becomes the I. L. Ellwood & Company of DeKalb, and Ellwood and Washburn increase production of barbed wire to 2.84 million pounds.

1877   Ellwood convinces railroad companies to fence their right-of-ways with barbed wire.

Gates forms his own company and begins producing and selling wire illegally.

The nation's total production of barbed wire is nearly 13 million pounds.

1878   I. L. Ellwood & Company produces 23 million pounds of barbed wire.

The nation's total production of barbed wire is over 26 million pounds.

1879   Ellwood now supplies fifty-nine railroad companies with barbed wire.

The barbed wire industry produces over 50 million pounds.

Thomas Edison urges Congress to protect patent rights and the patent system.

A bill banning barbed wire fences is introduced to the Texas legislature but fails to pass.

1880   Court decision in *Washburn & Moen Manufacturing Co. v. Haish* declares Haish in violation of Glidden's patent and of several other foundation patents owned by the company.

I. L. Ellwood & Company produces over 80 million pounds of barbed wire.

1881   Haish signs an agreement with I. L. Ellwood & Company assigning it his rights to the "S" barb and other patents in return for a license to manufacture and sell barbed wire, with royalty payments to be paid to the company.

The fence cutting wars break out.

The number of Texas longhorns driven to Kansas is only 267,000.

Cattlemen begin erecting drift fences on the open range to keep cattle from wandering too far south.

Glidden and Sanborn purchase 250,000 acres in the Texas panhandle and create the Frying Pan Ranch to demonstrate the utility of barbed wire to cattlemen.

1882   The federal government issues its first order for removal of all improvements, including barbed wire fences, from the Cherokee Outlet in Indian Territory. This order is largely ignored.

1883   The violence of the fence cutting wars peaks.

Construction of the XIT Ranch begins on 3,050,000 acres in the Texas Panhandle.

The U.S. land commissioner publishes a reminder to cattlemen that they have no right to erect fences on federally controlled land.

1884   A special session of the Texas legislature makes fence cutting a felony and erecting illegal fences a misdemeanor.

Proposal at the National Stockmen's Convention calls for cattlemen to purchase land and request government assistance for a national cattle trail.

1885   The U.S. government begins enforcing laws to quell the fence cutting violence. President Grover Cleveland orders all unlawful enclosures removed from public lands, directs the U.S. Marshal to send forces to take down illegal fences, and forbids threats and intimidations against settlers on public land.

A series of severe blizzards strikes the Great Plains during the winter of 1885–86, leading to the "Big Die-Up." Thousands of cattle die from the cold when drift fences prevent them from moving south.

I. L. Ellwood & Company sells barbed wire to over one hundred railroad companies.

U.S. Congress begins enforcing laws against fence cutting violence.

1887   Approximately ten million acres are illegally fenced as the practice reaches its peak.

The Dawes Act is passed, which breaks up Indian reservations into 160-acre parcels and allots the parcels to individual Indians rather than to tribes.

1890   The federal government issues a final order that all improvements—barbed wire fences and houses put up by cattlemen—be torn down on the Cherokee Outlet in Indian Territory and sends troops to enforce the order.

1892   The patent battles over barbed wire end with the United States Supreme Court's decision favoring Glidden and I. L. Ellwood & Company in *Washburn & Moen Manufacturing Co. et al. v. Beat 'Em All Barbed-Wire Company*, earning Glidden his title, "the Father of Barbed Wire."

1900   Population in the West numbers 17 million citizens. More than 600,000 claims, encompassing 80 million acres, have been filed under the Homestead Act.

1901   Barbed wire production in the United States is 135,000 tons.

1976   The Homestead Act is repealed after nearly four million homestead claims and the privatization of 270 million acres of public land—10 percent of all land in the country.

Glossary

cattleman. Cattle owner; one who is in the business of raising and selling cattle.

drift fences. Barbed wire fences erected in unconnected linear sections, intended to deter cattle from wandering out of the chosen range area.

free wire movement. Social-political movement that emerged in the mid-1870s favoring the use of illegally produced barbed wire, or "moonshine" wire, in response to the growing monopoly of Isaac L. Ellwood and Washburn & Moen Manufacturing Company.

Great American Desert. The geographical area of the United States roughly bordered by the Mississippi River on the east and the Rocky Mountains on the west, which, until the mid-1800s, many Americans believed was a vast desert.

Herd Law. Traditional belief and practice dictating that livestock owners fence in their stock to keep them from damaging neighbors' property. Herd law was the tradition in the eastern United States.

homestead. To acquire public land by filing a claim and then living on and cultivating the land.

Law of the Open Range. Traditional belief and practice allowing cattle free access to all waterways and grazing areas, regardless of who legally owned the property. Open range was the main tradition in the West.

line rider. A cowboy who patrolled a cattleman's ranch boundaries, especially during the winter, to keep the livestock from wandering too far south in inclement weather.

longhorn. The toughest breed of cattle in the United States, descended from cattle brought to the New World by the Spanish. The breed was capable of thriving in both bitter cold and brutal heat.

Manifest Destiny. The notion, made popular in the mid- and late-1800s, that it was America's destiny to settle the land from the Atlantic to the Pacific Oceans. Manifest Destiny was one idea used to justify the removal of Indians from their native homelands.

mavericks. Unbranded cattle wandering on the open range.

moonshine wire. Illegally produced barbed wire manufactured and sold without patent rights, typically at lower prices than wire produced by legally licensed manufacturers.

open range. Large tracts of land used freely, regardless of ownership, by cowboys for grazing and watering their livestock and by Indians for hunting and gathering.

plashing. A technique of cutting, bending, and intertwining hedge branches to create a barrier impervious to cattle.

preemption. The right to settle government land first and buy it later at a low cost. The call for preemption was particularly strong in the mid-1800s, when land ownership opportunities in the East were few.

relocation. The government's act of forcing Native Americans from their native lands to other areas.

right-of-way. The right to use land without owning it.

roundup. The periodic gathering, usually twice yearly, of cattle and of cattle owners. Cowboys herded the cattle that were roaming on the open range to one gathering spot, where cattlemen of the region sorted out stock ownership, branded their mavericks, and dealt with various range matters.

rustling. Stealing livestock and branding or altering the existing brand to indicate different ownership.

trail drive. The primary method of transporting cattle to eastern markets before the arrival and prominence of the railway in the American West. Cattle were driven for hundreds, sometimes thousands, of miles over prairies and plains to market.

vaquero. The Spanish cowboy, predecessor to the American cowboy. The vaquero's origins date back to the mid-1600s.

wrangler. Cowboy responsible for taking care of the saddle horses.

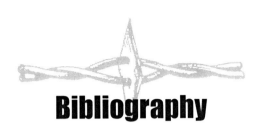

Bibliography

Anderson, H. Allen. "The Frying Pan Ranch." The Handbook of Texas Online, Texas State Historical Society, January 17, 2008. http://www.tshaonline.org/handbook/online/articles/FF/apf3.html.

———. "XIT Ranch." The Handbook of Texas Online, Texas State Historical Society, January 10, 2008. http://www.tshaonline.org/handbook/online/articles/XX/apx1.html.

Antique Barbed Wire Society. "Barbed Wire Inventors: Isaac Leonard Ellwood." Antique Barbed Wire Society, 2006. http://www.antiquebarbedwiresociety.com/inventors_ellwood.html.

———. "Barbed Wire Inventors: Joseph F. Glidden." Antique Barbed Wire Society, 2006. http://www.antiquebarbedwiresociety.com/inventors_glidden.html.

Bakken, Gordon Morris, ed. *Law in the Western United States.* Norman: University of Oklahoma Press, 2000.

Ball, Charles. "Cattle Industry History." National Cattlemen's Beef Association, 2008. http://www.beefusa.org/theicattleindustryhistory.aspx.

Beneke, Jeff. *The Fence Bible.* North Adams, Mass.: Storey Publishing, 2005.

Biggers, Don Hampton. *Buffalo Guns and Barbed Wire: Two Frontier Accounts*. Lubbock: Texas Tech University Press, 1991.

Blackmar, Frank W., ed. "Great American Desert." Kansas State Library, The KSGenWeb Project, http://skyways.lib.ks.us/genweb/archives/1912/g/great_american_desert.html. From *Kansas: a cyclopedia of state history, embracing events, institutions, industries, counties, cities, towns, prominent persons, etc.* Vol. 1, pp. 784–85. Chicago: Standard Publishing Co., 1912.

Blevins, Winfred. *Dictionary of the American West*. Seattle: Sasquatch Books, 2001.

Brintle, Sidney A. "Gates, John Warne." The Handbook of Texas Online, Texas State Historical Society, January 17, 2008. http://www.tshaonline.org/handbook/online/articles/GG/fga41.html.

Calvert, Robert A., Arnoldo De Leon, and Gregg Cantrell. *The History of Texas*. Wheeling, Ill.: Harlan Davidson, 2002.

Carlson, Paul H. *The Plains Indians*. College Station: Texas A&M University Press, 1998.

Carlson, Paul H., ed. *The Cowboy Way: An Exploration of History and Culture*. Lubbock: Texas Tech University Press, 2000.

Cashion, Ty. "Texas and the Western Frontier." Texas Beyond History, The University of Texas at Austin, 2006. http://www.texasbeyondhistory.net/forts/frontier.html.

———. *A Texas Frontier: The Clear Fork Country and Fort Griffin, 1849–1887*. Norman: University of Oklahoma Press, 1996.

Cook, Scott. "The Development and Rise of Barbed Wire." American Studies at the University of Virginia, 2006. http://xroads.virginia.edu/~CLASS/am485_98/cook/develp.htm.

———. "The Introduction of Barbed Wire to the Frontier." American Studies at the University of Virginia, 2006. http://xroads.virginia.edu/~CLASS/am485_98/cook/develp2.htm.

Ellwood House Association. "History of Barbed Wire—Fencing Frontiers: The Barbed Wire Story." The Ellwood House Association, 2004. http://www.ellwoodhouse.org/barb _wire/index.html.

Gates, Paul W. *The History of Public Land Law Development*. New York: Arno Press, 1979.

Grace, Jim W. "The Enduring Osage Orange." *Missouri Conservationist Online*, Vol. 56, no. 11, November 1995. http://mdc.mo.gov/conmag/1995/11/06.html.

Greever, William S. *Arid Domain*. New York: Arno Press, 1979.

Hagemeier, Harold. *The Barbed Wire Identification Encyclopedia*. Kearney, Neb.: Morris Publishing, 1998.

Haley, J. Evetts. *The XIT Ranch of Texas: And the Early Days of the Llano Estacado*. Norman: University of Oklahoma Press, 1929.

Hayter, Earl W. "Barbed Wire Fencing—A Prairie Invention: Its Rise and Influence in the Western States." http://xroads. virginia.edu/~UG99/cook/barb1.htm. From *Agricultural History*, Vol. 13, October 1939.

Higgs, Robert. "How the Western Cattlemen Created Property Rights." Independent Institute, March 1, 2005. http://www .independent.org/publications/article.asp?id=1491.

Iowa State Agricultural Society. *Seventh Annual Report of the Iowa State Agricultural Society, to the Governor of the State, for the Year 1860*. Des Moines, Iowa: F.W. Palmer, State Printer, 1961.

Keating, Bern. *Famous American Cowboys: Where Did the Cowboy Come From?* New York: Rand McNally & Company, 1977.

Kingston, Mike. *A Concise History of Texas*. Houston: Gulf Publishing Company, 1988.

Lauber, Patricia. *Cowboys and Cattle Ranching: Yesterday and Today*. New York: Thomas Y. Crowell Company, 1973.

Love, Clara M. "History of the Cattle Industry in the South-West." Vol. 019, no. 4, *Southwestern Historical Quarterly Online,* http://www.tshaonline.org/publications/journals/shq/online/v019/n4/article_2.html.

Malin, James C. *Winter Wheat in the Golden Belt of Kansas: A Study in Adaptation to Subhumid Geographical Environment.* Lawrence: University of Kansas Press, 1944. Online at Kansas State Library, The KSGenWeb Project, http://skyways.lib.ks.us/orgs/fordco/malin/.

McCallum, Henry D., and Frances T. McCallum. *The Wire that Fenced the West.* Norman: University of Oklahoma Press, 1965.

Montejano, David. *Anglos and Mexicans in the Making of Texas, 1836–1986.* Austin: University of Texas Press, 1987.

National Council on Economic Education. "Why Don't Cowboys Ever Ride into the Sunset?" United States History: Focus on Economics. http://www.ncee.net/resources/lessons/Focus_US_History_Sample_Lesson.pdf.

National Inventors Hall of Fame. "Joseph Glidden." Invent Now, 2002. http://www.invent.org/hall_of_fame/269.html.

Nebraska State Historical Society. "Nebraska Trailblazer #1: American Indians, Background Information." http://www.nebraskahistory.org/museum/teachers/material/trail/indians/backgrnd.htm.

Carey, H. C., and I. Lea. *A Complete Historical, Chronological, and Geographical American Atlas, Being a Guide to the History of North and South America, and the West Indies . . . to the Year 1822.* Philadelphia: H. C. Carey & I. Lea, 1822.

New York Times. "John W. Gates, The Greatest of American Plungers." July 16, 1911. http://query.nytimes.com/gst/abstract.html?res=9D01E3DE1131E233A25755C1A9619C946096D6CF.

Office of the Governor (Texas), Economic Development and Tourism. "XIT Ranch." TravelTex, Official Site of Texas Tourism, 2008. http://www.traveltex.com/pg/Activity.aspx?id = 49af78ce-a349-4d14-b5da-7284e9532f61.

Ohio Historical Society. "Lucien B. Smith." Ohio History Central, 2006. http://www.ohiohistorycentral.org/entry.php?rec = 2672.

OKGenWeb. "Day County, Oklahoma Territory, from 1892 to 1907, had controversy and trouble." Oklahoma Genealogy and History, OKGenWeb, 2008. http://www.okgenweb.org/~day/.

Oklahoma History Museum. "The Long Cattle Drive." Oklahoma History Center, 2008. http://www.okhistorycenter.org/index.php?option = com_content&task = view&id = 81&Itemid = 111.

Olmsted, Frederick Law. Olmsted's Texas Journey. New York: Dix, Edwards & Co., 1857.

Pelta, Kathy. Cattle Trails: "Git Along Little Dogies. Austin, Tex.: Raintree Steck-Vaughn Publishers, 1997.

Place, Marian T. American Cattle Trails East and West. New York: Holt, Rinehart and Winston, Inc., 1967.

Potter, Lee Ann, and Wynell Schamel. "The Homestead Act of 1862." Social Education, Vol. 61, no. 6 (October 1997): 359–364. Online at U.S. National Archives and Records Administration, Teaching with Documents, http://www.archives.gov/education/lessons/homestead-act/.

Public Broadcasting Service. "Archives of the West 1868–1874: The Pacific Railway Act, July 1, 1862." New Perspectives on the West, The West Film Project, 2001. http://www.pbs.org/weta/thewest/resources/archives/five/railact.htm.

———. "Events in the West 1860-1870." New Perspectives on the West, The West Film Project and WETA, 2001. http://www.pbs.org/weta/thewest/events/1860_1870.htm.

Ray, Emily, and Wynell Schamel. "Glidden's Patent Application for Barbed Wire." *Social Education*, Vol. 61, no. 1 (January 1997): 52–55. Online at U.S. National Archives and Records Administration, Teaching with Documents, http://www.archives.gov/education/lessons/barbed-wire/.

Razac, Olivier. *Barbed Wire: A Political History*. Translated by Jonathan Kneight. New York: New Press, 2000.

Robbins, Roy M. *Our Landed Heritage: The Public Domain, 1776–1936*. Lincoln: University of Nebraska Press, 1942. Online at Digital Text International, http://www.ditext.com/robbins/land.html.

Ross, Nelson. "Free Grass vs. Fences." Navarro County (Texas) Historical Society, TXGenWeb. Originally published in the Navarro County Scroll, 1967. http://www.txgenweb6.org/txnavarro/business/cattle_industry/free_grass_vs_fences.htm.

Saunders, George. "The Early Days: Over the Chisholm Trail in the '60s." *The Cattleman*, Vol. 1, no. 2 (March 1915). Online at Texas and Southwestern Cattle Raisers Association, http://www.thecattlemanmagazine.com/earlyDays/earlychisholmtrail.asp.

Schultz, Stanley K., and William P. Tishler. "Civil War to the Present: Which Old West and Whose?" American History 102, University of Wisconsin System Board of Regents, 2004. http://us.history.wisc.edu/hist102/weblect/lec03/03_02.htm.

Schumacher, M. J. "Hooked on Barbed Wire?" *The Bandera Bulletin*, August 3, 2004. http://www.banderabulletin.com/articles/2005/10/25/news/cowboy/story05.txt.

Shannon, Fred Albert. *The Farmer's Last Frontier: Agriculture, 1860–1897*. Armonk, NY: M.E. Sharpe, Inc., 1977.

Sheldon, Addison Erwin. "History and Stories of Nebraska: The Herd Law." Oldtime Nebraska, 2008. http://www.olden-times.com/oldtimenebraska/n-csnyder/nbstory/story43.html.

Smithsonian National Museum of American History. "Barbed Wire, the Thorny Fence that Transformed the West." Lemelson Center for the Study of Invention and Innovation, 2006. http://www.inventionatplay.org/inventors_bar.html#.

Starrs, Paul F. *Let the Cowboy Ride: Cattle Ranching in the American West*. Baltimore: Johns Hopkins University Press, 1998.

Stefeffo, Rebecca. *American Voices from the Wild West*. New York: Marshall Cavendish Benchmark, 2007.

Torr, James D., ed. *Westward Expansion*. Farmington Hills, Mich.: Greenhaven Press, 2003.

Trew, Delbert. "A Brief History of Barbed Wire." Devil's Rope Museum, 2007. http://www.barbwiremuseum.com/barbedwirehistory.htm.

University of Kentucky. "A Brief Explanation of Historical Patterns of Population Change: The Settlement of the Great Plains in America." Agripedia, University of Kentucky College of Agriculture, 2006. http://www.ca.uky.edu/Agripedia/Classes/archived/GEN100/POPBSET.asp.

University of Oregon and Eugene School District 4J. "The Economy of the West after the Civil War." Chap. 16 in Problem Solving Through History, 2003. http://www.brtprojects.org/cyberschool/history/ch16/16questions.pdf.

U.S. Department of the Interior, National Park Service. "About the Homestead Act." Homestead National Monument of America, 2006. http://www.nps.gov/home/historyculture/abouthomesteadactlaw.htm.

———. "Exhibit Glossary." Jefferson National Expansion Memorial, National Park Service, 2006. http://www.nps.gov/jeff/planyourvisit/exhibit-glossary.htm.

———. "Frederick Law Olmsted." Frederick Law Olmsted National Historic Site, National Park Service, 2006. http://www.nps.gov/frla/.

———. "Migration and Settlement from the Atlantic to the Pacific, 1750-1890: A Survey of the Literature." By Kim M. Gruenwald, National Park Service, 2008. http://www.nps.gov/history/history/resedu/settlement.htm.

U.S. Fish and Wildlife Service. "American buffalo (*Bison bison*)." Species Accounts, U.S. Fish and Wildlife Service, January 1998. http://www.fws.gov/species/species_accounts/bio_buff.html.

U.S. Library of Congress. "The Homestead Act Went into Effect May 20, 1862." America's Story from America's Library, 2008. http://www.americaslibrary.gov/cgi-bin/page.cgi/jb/civil/homested_1.

Webb, Walter Prescott. *The Great Plains*. Lincoln: University of Nebraska Press, 1931.

Wheeler, Daniel L. "Panhandle Drift Fences." The Handbook of Texas Online, Texas State Historical Society, January 18, 2008. http://www.tshaonline.org/handbook/online/articles/PP/aoput.html.

White, Richard. *It's Your Misfortune and None of My Own: A New History of the American West*. Norman: University of Oklahoma Press, 1993.

Wolfgang, Otto. "The Early Days: How the Wild West Was Fenced In." *The Cattleman*, Vol. 53, no. 3 (August 1966). Online at Texas and Southwestern Cattle Raisers Association, http://www.thecattlemanmagazine.com/earlyDays/earlywestfenced.asp.

Woten, Rick L. "American Agriculture and the Development of a Nation's Land Policy." American Agricultural History Primer, Center for Agricultural History and Rural Studies, Iowa State University, 2008. http://www.history.iastate.edu/agprimer/Page12.html.

Writers' Program of the Work Projects Administration in the State of Wyoming, comps. "Timeline of Wyoming History." From *Wyoming, A Guide to Its History, Highways, and People*, American Guide Series, sponsored by Dr. Lester C. Hunt, Secretary of State, Oxford University Press, New York, 1941. Online at WYGENWEB Project, January 2009, http://wygenweb.org/timeline.htm.

XIT Museum. "History of the XIT Ranch." Dallam-Hartley Counties Historical Association, 2006. http://www.xitmuseum.com/history.shtml.

Index

Brighton Ranch, *57*, 104
buffalo, 1–2, *52*, 52, 94–95
Burlington & Missouri River Railroad
   Co., *74*

California, 3, 9, 19, 74
Carlsson, C. F., 22
cattle breeds, 3–4
cattle drives, 14–17, 53, 77–78, 84–86,
   95–98
cattle herds, *91*; barbed wire fences,
   53, 79–85; Civil War era, 12–13;
   drift fences, 80–81; grazing lands,
   6–7, 51–53, 82; Great Plains, 3, 4–5;
   tick-borne diseases, 85; weather
   conditions, 79–83
cattle industry: barbed wire fences,
   52–53, 109–11; breeding practices,
   110–11; cattle-raising operations, 4–5;
   Cherokee Outlet, *95*, 95–98; Civil
   War era, 12–13; lawlessness, 99–106;
   livestock losses, 75, 81–83; livestock
   markets, 13, 14, 16–17, 25, 53, 77;
   move to far West, 79; railroads, 14,
   16–17, 72, 75, 77; ranches, 88–90, *91*,
   108–11; Texas, 4, 13–14, 44–45
cattlemen. *See* cattle owners
cattle owners: barbed wire fences,
   52–53, 87–90, *91*, 109–11; big
   cattlemen–small cattlemen conflict,
   99, 104–5; cattle industry, 4–6;
   cattlemen-farmer power struggle,
   23–25, 44–45, 55–61, 100–104;
   conflict with railroad companies,
   75–77; fading traditions, 84–88;
   false claims, 99–100, 105; feed
   crops, *109*, 109–10; fence cutting
   wars, 55–61, *57*, 103–6; Herd Law,
   24; lawlessness, 99–106; opposition
   to barbed wire fences, 83; post-
   Civil War era, 13, 14; transition to
   ranching, 108–11, *109*
cattle thieves and rustlers, 14, 58, 105
cattle trails, *15*, 77–78, 84–86, 95–98
Central Pacific Railroad Company,
   73–74
Cherokee Outlet, *95*, 95–98
Cherokees, 92, 95–98
Cherokee Strip Livestock Association, 96

Cheyenne, Wyoming, 17
Cheyennes, 2
Chicago & North Western Railway, *78*
Chickasaws, 92
Chisholm Trail, *15*, 17
Choctaws, 92
chuckwagon, 16
Civil War, 10–13
Cleveland, Grover, 105
Colorado: cattle drives, 17, 77; cattle
   industry, 79; fence cutting wars, 58;
   Herd Law, 24; illegal fences, 56, 100;
   railroad right-of-ways, 75
Comanches, 2, 11, *93*
Confederacy, 12. *See also* Civil War
Connecticut, 53
cowboys, 5, *85*, *87*; barbed wire fences,
   52–53; cattle drives, 17, 77–78;
   cattle-raising techniques, 5–6; Civil
   War era, 12–13; fading traditions,
   84–88; fence cutting wars, 56–61;
   history, 5–6; line riders, 79–80;
   post–Civil War era, 14
coyotes, 82
Creeks, 92
crops, 10
Crows, 2
Custer County, Nebraska, 104

Dabb, Alphonso, 36
Dakota Territory, 82, 86
Dawes General Allotment Act (1887), 98
DeKalb, Illinois, 34, 36–37, *42*, 42–44, 49
DeKalb County Fair, 37, 40, 42
Desert Land Act (1877), 101
devil's rope, 51–52, 83
Devon cattle, 3
dirt ridges, 29
disease, 2
ditches, 29
Dodge City, Kansas, 17, 86
Donation Land Law (1850), 19
drift fences, 80–83
drought, 9, 28, 82

East, the: ban on barbed wire, 53;
   barbed wire factories, 63, *71*; cattle
   herds, 4, 32; emigration to the West,
   18; fences, 24, 31–32; grain demand,

National Convention of Cattleman (1884), 85–86

Native Americans: barbed wire fences, 51–52, 92–98; buffalo hunting, 2; Cherokee Outlet, *95*, 95–98; conflict with cattlemen and cowboys, 6; loss of land, 98; nomadic traditions, 2, 92–93; raids on white settlements, 11–12; relocations, 2, 92–94

Nebraska: ban on barbed wire, 54; barbed wire factories, 67; fence cutting wars, *57*, 104; Herd Law Act (1870), 24; homesteaders, *22*, 22; Plains Indians, 51; population growth, 79; railroad right-of-ways, 75; railroads, 73; settlement, *74*; soil ridges, 29; stone fields, 28

New Hampshire, 53

New Mexico Territory: cattle drives, 17, 77; cattle industry, 14; illegal fences, 56; Indian raids, 11; post–Civil War government control, 12

New Orleans, Louisiana, 16, 77

Oklahoma: Cherokee Outlet, 98; Indian raids, 11; Plains Indians, 51

Olmsted, Frederick Law, 1

Omaha, Nebraska, 73

open range: barbed wire fences, 52–53; cattle drives, 17, 77–78; cattlemen-farmer power struggle, 23–25, 44–45, 55–61; enforcement policies, 17; fading traditions, 84–86; farming activities, 23–25; Herd Law, 23–25; overcrowding, 86–87; railroads, 72, 77–78; unwritten laws, 6–7, 13

Oregon Territory, 8, 9, 19

Osage orange hedges, *30*, 30, 42–43

Osnabrock, North Dakota, *109*

Pacific Railway Act (1862), 73–75

Panhandle, the Texas, 79–83, 88–90

patents: barbed wire fences, 35–37, 63, 83; disputes, 48, 62–63; Ellwood's barbed wire design, *41*, 41; fences, 34; French patents, 35; Glidden's barbed wire design, *38*, *39*, 40; Haish's "S" barb design, 42–43, *43*; Hunt's revolving wheel design, *36*;

legal rights, 68–69; Rose's barbed wire design, *37*; U.S. patents, *38*, *39*, 63, 83; violations, 66–69

Peoria, Illinois, 35

Pike, Zebulon, 8

Plains Indians, 2, 51–52, 92–94

plashing technique, 30, 31

political tactics, 101–2

prairie fires, 28, 31

prairie grasslands, 1–2, 6, 8

Preemption Act (1841), 18–19

Promontory, Utah, 74

pronghorns, 2

property damage, 59, 104

property rights, 7

public lands: barbed wire fences, 52–53, 60, 100; cattle herds, 7; cattlemen-farmer power struggle, 44–45, 56–61; false claims, 99–100; illegal fences, 100, 103–6

Pueblo Indians, 94

rail fences. *See* wood fences

railroads, *15*; barbed wire fences, 72, 76–78; cattle industry, 14, 16–17, 72, 77; end of the frontier, 78; federal legislation, 73–75; fence construction, 75–77; livestock losses, 75; open range, 72, 77–78; right-of-ways, 23, 75–77; western settlements, *74*, 74–75

ranches, 88–90, *91*, 108–11

real estate speculators, 23

reservation, Indian, 2, 92–94

ridges, 29

rodents, 31

Roosevelt, Theodore, 82, 106

Rose, Henry M., 37

roundups, 14

rustlers, 14, 58, 105

Sacramento, California, 74

San Antonio, Texas, 45–48

Sanborn, Henry B., 44–45, 88

"S" barb design, 42–43, *43*, 70

schoolhouse, *111*

Sedalia, Missouri, 16, 17

Seminoles, 92

settlements. *See* western settlements

About the Author

Joanne S. Liu is a Texas-based freelance writer who has published articles in *The History Channel Magazine*, *Learning Through History Magazine*, and *History Magazine*, among others. After receiving a bachelor of arts from Brown and a law degree from Boston University, she practiced law in New England, where she specialized in tracing ownership of real estate back to the 1700s. She now resides in Houston, Texas, with her husband and daughter.

CPSIA information can be obtained
at www.ICGtesting.com
Printed in the USA
FSOW02n0155090316
17679FS